THE LUCID DREAMING MIND

How To Control Your Dreams, Break Through The Walls Of Sleep And Get Into Complete Mind-Body Awareness

Melissa Gomes

>> https://smartpa.ge/MelissaGomes<<

Table of Contents

TABLE OF CONTENTS   3

FREEBIES!   7

BONUS 1: FREE WORKBOOK - VALUE 12.95$ 7
BONUS 2: FREE BOOK - VALUE 12.95$ 8
BONUS 3: FREE AUDIOBOOK - VALUE 14.95$ 8
JOIN MY REVIEW TEAM!   8
FOR ALL THE FREEBIES, VISIT THE FOLLOWING LINK: 9

I'M HERE BECAUSE OF YOU   10

CHAPTER 1: INTRODUCTION TO LUCID DREAMING   11

WHAT IS LUCID DREAMING?   11
IS IT POSSIBLE TO CONTROL A DREAM?   13
THE SCIENCE OF LUCID DREAMING   14

CHAPTER 2: THE BENEFITS OF LUCID DREAMING   17

IMPROVE YOUR MOOD   17
BOOST YOUR CREATIVITY AND PROBLEM-SOLVING SKILLS   18
ENHANCE YOUR EMOTIONAL INTELLIGENCE   19
HEAL YOURSELF FROM TRAUMA AND ANXIETY   21
OVERCOME YOUR FEARS   22
IMPROVE YOUR PHYSICAL HEALTH   23
CONNECT WITH YOUR SPIRITUALITY   24
    What Is Spirituality?   *24*
    How Can Lucid Dreaming Help You Connect with Your Spirituality?   *25*
EXPERIENCE LUCID LIVING   25

CHAPTER 3: RISKS OF LUCID DREAMING   27

SLEEP PARALYSIS   27
    Sleep Paralysis Symptoms: *27*
    Causes of Sleep Paralysis: *28*
    Risk Factors for Sleep Paralysis: *28*
FALSE AWAKENINGS   28
SLEEP DEPRIVATION   30
UNWANTED NIGHTMARES   31
WAKING LIFE CONFUSION   33
INCREASED ANXIETY   35
    Anxiety Disorders: *36*

How to prevent or manage increased anxiety while lucid dreaming   *36*
ISOLATION AND HALLUCINATIONS   37

CHAPTER 4: GET READY FOR LUCID DREAMING   **40**

SLEEP HABITS AND DREAMS   40
THE FOUR STAGES OF SLEEP   41
MAINTAIN POSITIVE SLEEP HABITS   43
SLEEP HYGIENE   44
  Keep Healthy Sleep Habits   *44*
  Keep a good Sleep Hygiene.   *45*
RECALLING YOUR DREAMS   47
PREPARE FOR DREAM JOURNALING   49
PRACTICE: CREATE YOUR DREAM JOURNAL   52
SET YOUR LUCID DREAMING GOALS   53
  Setting your lucid dreaming goals tips: *55*

CHAPTER 5: LUCID DREAMING TECHNIQUES   **57**

MNEMONIC INDUCTION OF LUCID DREAMS (MILD)   57
  How it Works   *58*
TIPS FOR USING MNEMONIC INDUCTION OF LUCID DREAMS   58
THE WAKE INITIATED LUCID DREAM (WILD) TECHNIQUE   60
WAKE BACK TO BED   62
  Tips for Using Wake Back to Bed   *63*
THE FULFILMENT BOX   64
THE SYMBOL TECHNIQUE   65
REALITY CHECKS   66
VISUALIZATIONS   68
AUTOSUGGESTION   69
DREAM REENTRY   70
KEEPING A DREAM DIARY   71
  Tips for keeping a dream journal.   *72*

CHAPTER 6: PREPARING FOR YOUR FIRST LUCID DREAM EXPERIENCE   **74**

PUT YOURSELF IN THE RIGHT FRAME OF MIND   74
SELECT A LUCIDITY TECHNIQUE THAT SUITS YOU   77
CREATE A DREAM-FRIENDLY ENVIRONMENT.   79
BE PREPARED FOR SETBACKS.   80
SET ASIDE YOUR EXPECTATIONS.   82
LOOK FOR PROGRESS RATHER THAN PERFECTION.   83
REWARD YOURSELF FOR YOUR ACCOMPLISHMENTS.   85

CHAPTER 7: INSIDE A LUCID DREAM   **87**

STRONGER LUCIDITY 87
  Exercise control 90
  Practice changing your dreams 90
  Increase positive emotions 91
  Skill rehearsal 92
  Creative problem solving 92
INCREASED SELF-INTEGRATION 93
LUCID DREAMING IN REAL LIFE 96
  Parallels 96
  Take control of your mind 97
  Set intentions 98

CHAPTER 8: DEALING WITH FEAR IN LUCID DREAMS **100**

  UNDERSTANDING THE FEAR-MOTIVATED BEHAVIOR IN LUCID DREAMS 100
  COUNTERING THE FEAR-MOTIVATED BEHAVIOR 102
  WORKING WITH FEAR IN LUCID DREAMS 104
  TRANSFORMING NIGHTMARES WITH LUCID DREAMING 105
  HOW TO RESPOND TO NIGHTMARES 107

POSITIVE AFFIRMATIONS – PART 1 .... **109**

POSITIVE AFFIRMATIONS – PART 2 .... **113**

GUIDED MEDITATION **116**

FREEBIES! **120**

  BONUS 1: FREE WORKBOOK - VALUE 12.95$ 120
  BONUS 2: FREE BOOK - VALUE 12.95$ 121
  BONUS 3: FREE AUDIOBOOK - VALUE 14.95$ 121
  JOIN MY REVIEW TEAM! 121
  FOR ALL THE FREEBIES, VISIT THE FOLLOWING LINK: 122

I'M HERE BECAUSE OF YOU **123**

FREEBIES

AND

RELATED PRODUCTS

WORKBOOKS
AUDIOBOOKS
FREE BOOKS
REVIEW COPIES

HERE

HTTPS://SMARTPA.GE/MELISSAGOMES

Freebies!

I have a **special treat for you**! You can access exclusive bonuses I created specifically for my readers at the following link! The link will redirect you to a webpage containing all my books and bonuses for each book. Just select the book you have purchased and check the bonuses!

>> https://smartpa.ge/MelissaGomes<<

OR scan the QR Code with your phone's camera

Bonus 1: Free Workbook - Value 12.95$

This **workbook** will guide you with **specific questions** and give you all the space you need to write down the answers. Taking time for **self-reflection** is extremely valuable, especially when looking to develop new skills and **learn** new concepts. I highly suggest you ***grab this complimentary workbook for yourself***, as it will help you gain clarity on your goals. Some authors like to sell the workbook, but I think giving it away for free is the perfect way to say **"thank you" to my readers**.

Bonus 2: Free Book - Value 12.95$

Grab a **free short book** with **22+ Techniques for Meditation**. The book will introduce you to a range of meditation practices you can use to help you develop your inner awareness, inner calm, and overall sense of well-being. You will also learn how to begin a meditation practice that works for you regardless of your schedule. These meditation techniques work for everyone, regardless of age or fitness level. Check it out at the link below!

Bonus 3: Free audiobook - Value 14.95$

If you love listening to audiobooks on the go or would enjoy a narration as you read along, I have great news for you. You can download the audiobook version of *my books* for **FREE** just by signing up for a FREE 30-day trial! You can find the audio versions of my books (depending on availability) at the following link.

Join my Review Team!

Are you an avid reader looking to have more insights into spirituality? Do you want to get free books in exchange for an honest review? You can do so by joining my Review Team! You will get priority access to my books before they are released. You only need to follow me on Booksprout, and you will get notified every time a new Review Copy is available for my latest release!

For all the Freebies, visit the following link:

>> https://smartpa.ge/MelissaGomes<<

OR scan the QR Code with your phone's camera.

I'm here because of you

When you're supporting an independent author,
you're supporting a dream. Please leave
an honest review by scanning
the QR code below and clicking on the "Leave a Review" Button.

https://smartpa.ge/MelissaGomes

Chapter 1: Introduction to Lucid Dreaming

What is Lucid dreaming?

Lucid dreaming is a type of dream in which the individual is aware that they are dreaming. In some cases, individuals may be able to control their dreams and influence the dream content. Lucid dreaming can occur spontaneously, or specific techniques may induce it. Sleepwalking is a similar parasomnia characterized by transient confusion between sleep and waking, while with hypnagogic hallucinations, there is a waking-like experience in the transition between sleep and wakefulness.

A person with lucid dreams for the first time will often find it frightening. However, some people find it less bothersome than others, and some claim to enjoy lucid dreaming. Lucid dreaming typically involves an experience of dream control. However, people disagree as to whether dream control really occurs or whether the experience is simply that of an illusion of control.

There are many different types of dreams, ranging from simple daydreams to full-blown nightmares. Lucid dreams fall somewhere between these two extremes; while they can be vivid and realistic like a nightmare, the individual is aware that they are dreaming and can often exert some control over the dream content. Because of this awareness, lucid dreams have been studied extensively by both scientists and spiritual practitioners as a way to understand consciousness and explore human potential.

Most people will experience at least one episode of lucid dreaming in their lifetime without any training or effort required on their part – although only around 20% report having them frequently. For most people, spontaneous lucid dreams tend to occur during adolescence – although there is no definitive explanation for why this age group seems to experience them more frequently than other adults.

However, if you would like to increase your chances of experiencing a lucid dream spontaneously, there are certain things you can do before bed that may help. Meditation, visualization, and sleep hygiene can all help increase your chances of lucid dreaming.

There are a variety of different techniques that can help you learn to become a lucid dreamer. These techniques fall into two general categories: those that train your brain to expect lucidity and those that trigger lucidity directly.

In contrast to spontaneous lucid dreams, induced lucid dreams occur due to specific techniques being carried out to induce lucidity. While there is some debate surrounding the most effective method for doing this, the consensus is that it is possible to learn how to have an induced lucid dream with sufficient practice. Generally speaking, the process involves relaxing your body and mind completely before entering into REM sleep – at which point you "program" yourself to become aware during dreaming by repeating affirmations or visualizing particular dream scenarios.

Lucid dreaming can be a fun and exciting way to explore your consciousness and experience things that would otherwise be impossible. However, it should be noted that some risks are associated with lucidity, such as losing touch with reality or experiencing frightening or negative dream scenarios.

As long as these risks are kept in mind and steps are taken to avoid them, there is no reason why anyone shouldn't enjoy experimenting with this fascinating state of consciousness.

Is it possible to Control a Dream?

While it is possible to remain aware while dreaming, it isn't always guaranteed that you'll experience lucid dreams. Some people successfully remember being aware while dreaming, while others only recall fragments of their dreams. Although it's possible to become lucid during a dream, some people experience lucidity without remembering being aware while asleep. Some of the common ways to become lucid include:

Reality checks: If you conduct reality checks throughout the day, you train your mind to become more aware of your surroundings and when it's asleep or awake. Many lucid dreaming techniques involve carrying out reality checks during the day or just before sleep to become more self-aware when dreaming and conscious.

Stimulating the senses: During a dream, your perception can be heightened, and you may hear or see things more clearly than when awake. Inducing lucid dreams through sensory stimulation, such as listening to loud, repetitive music or taking a shower before bed, can help trigger lucidity and make you more aware of your environment and perceptions.

Sleep deprivation: Keeping yourself awake for long periods increases the chances of experiencing lucidity while asleep.

Meditation: Meditation techniques like the Vajrasattva meditation can help you become aware of your consciousness while asleep.

Visualizing yourself becoming lucid during a particular scenario: By visualizing a particular situation or setting in which you believe you can become lucid, you can train your mind to become aware that you are dreaming in such a situation.

Although it is possible to control dream content to some extent, it's usually easier to increase your chances of entering a dream state or becoming lucid by training your mind to become more aware of your surroundings throughout the day or before sleep.

The Science of Lucid Dreaming

Lucid dreaming has been a topic of scientific study for over a hundred years, and there is now a wealth of research to support the existence of this state of consciousness. In recent years, technological advances have allowed scientists to further explore the physiology of lucid dreaming and how it relates to other states of sleep and wakefulness. Science has also revealed that while dreaming and being aware are two separate phenomenons, awareness of these different states of consciousness can enhance them both.

Although it is impossible to alter one state of consciousness without affecting another, you can become more fully aware of your consciousness while you are dreaming. This means that you may be able to take advantage of certain benefits associated with dreaming while being aware of your conscious state simultaneously.

During REM sleep, the brainwave activity increases during sleep paralysis and increases simultaneously as the dreamer becomes aware of the dream state. The amygdala activity also increased when the dreamer became aware during REM sleep. The amygdala is an important brain region responsible for the fear and emotion systems.

While the exact mechanisms behind lucid dreaming are still not fully understood, there is evidence to suggest that it is associated with changes in brain activity during REM sleep – when most dreams occur. It is also thought that individuals who can have lucid dreams more frequently tend to have greater self-awareness during waking life and be more "in touch" with their subconscious minds.

Lucid dreaming occurs during REM sleep, which is when most dreams occur. During REM sleep, the brainwave activity is similar to wakefulness, but there are also some notable differences. For example, eye movements are suppressed, and muscle activity is greatly reduced. It is thought that these changes in brain activity may be associated with the vividness and bizarreness of dream content.

In addition to changes in brain activity, lucid dreaming is also associated with several physiological changes – such as an increase in heart rate and blood pressure. These changes are thought to be caused by the activation of the sympathetic nervous system during REM sleep.

The most important thing to remember about inducing lucidity is that it should never be attempted while sleepy or tired. This can lead to dangerous situations where you may fall asleep without meaning and enter a regular dream state. Instead, it's best to attempt lucidity induction techniques when feeling wide awake and well-rested.

There are many different methods for inducing Lucid Dreams. Still, they all rely on two general principles: firstly, you need to train your mind to expect lucidity, and secondly, you need to create conditions that trigger awareness during dreaming.

Some of the most popular methods for inducing lucidity include:

- Mnemonic induction of lucid dreams: This technique was developed by Stephen LaBerge and essentially involved repeating a "lucidity trigger" phrase to yourself just before falling asleep to become aware during dreaming.
- **Wake back to bed**: This method involves setting an alarm clock to wake you up after 4-6 hours of sleep, at which point you stay awake for 30 minutes to an hour before going back to bed. During this time, it is recommended that you do some mental activity such as reading or working on a puzzle, anything that will help keep your mind active. The theory behind this method is that it allows you to enter into REM sleep with a higher level of cognitive awareness, making lucidity more likely.

- **Sleep paralysis**: Induce sleep paralysis by waking yourself up on purpose or buzzing yourself awake while falling asleep. Once you become conscious again, it's common to experience strong muscle paralysis and the feeling that you are awake but unable to move. This is the point where many people experience lucid dreams. Sometimes just becoming aware of the paralysis is enough to induce lucid dreaming; other times, you will need to deliberately try to enter a dream state.
- **Dream journaling**: This is a very popular technique that involves writing about your experience in a dream as soon as you wake up. Discussing your dream in detail can encourage your subconscious to remember it later and make you more likely to recall the dream while sleeping in the future.
- **Dream incubation**: This lucid dreaming technique involves reviewing dreams and replaying them in your mind before you go to sleep. The aim is to encourage your subconscious to remember the dream and produce emotions or sensations similar to the dream's content once you fall asleep. To make the dream more vivid, you should repeat out loud any phrases or words that you recall from the dream.

Chapter 2: The Benefits of Lucid Dreaming

Lucid dreaming isn't just about remembering your dreams or predicting what will happen in your dream. There are real benefits to training our minds to become lucid in our dreams.

Improve Your Mood

Lucid dreaming can help you process and work through difficult emotions like stress, anxiety, or depression. The more you practice lucid dreaming, the more ready your mind becomes to experience more positive emotions and deal with difficult circumstances. Lucid dreaming healthily helps your brain process emotions rather than staying stuck in agitated or anxious thoughts or emotional spirals. It can also help you work out old emotional baggage to move forward and live the life you want.

By understanding your emotions in your dreams, you can learn to integrate them into your daily life. With practice, you can learn how to control your emotional response to stress or anxiety and reframe negative thought patterns into more positive affirmations. This can help you become more optimistic in life.

With lucid dreaming, you feel more relaxed, peaceful, and accepting of yourself so you can move away from negative emotions and live a fuller, happier life. Lucid dreaming can also be used as a therapy to work through repressed memories and traumatic experiences. Many nightmares can be triggered by repressed emotions that haven't been dealt with or forgotten about. By facing these emotions and learning to deal with them constructively, you can release the painful feelings and healthily work through them.

You will explore different aspects of your personality so that you can understand yourself better and deal with any problems you may be going through. Using lucid dreaming to improve your mood can also lead to better sleep and improved focus throughout your day.

Boost Your Creativity and Problem-Solving Skills

Thanks to Lucid dreaming, you access the creative side of your consciousness and solve problems more intuitively. You will be able to solve problems and be more innovative in your daily life. Creativity is the ability to generate new ideas or information to adapt to a particular situation or problem. While it is about having original ideas, creativity can be enhanced and amplified by lucid dreaming.

Since lucid dreaming is an altered state of consciousness, it can open your mind to new possibilities. Viewing things from a higher perspective can enable your mind to think more freely and creatively and come up with fresh ideas that you may not have considered before. Since lucid dreaming triggers similar brain patterns as when we are awake, we can also become more creative in our waking life.

Lucid dreaming helps you explore solutions to problems in novel ways and think outside the box to find the best solutions. This can help you problem-solve more intuitively and improve your critical thinking skills.

You can use lucid dreaming to brainstorm ideas and solutions to problems in your daily life. Lucid dreaming can enable you to come up with creative solutions when you are stuck in a rut or on a problem you can't seem to push through.

Access forgotten memories and thoughts from the past so you can deal with them healthily. Accessing your subconscious mind can also enable you to solve problems from the past that may be holding you back or causing problems in your relationships or decision-making process.

Lucid dreaming can also help you make better decision choices in the future by helping you envision potential repercussions that hinge on your decision. By seeing the future versions of yourself, you can learn to make better and healthier decisions in the present.

You can practice skills in your dreams, leading to improved performance in your waking life. Lucid dreaming is a great way to learn and practice new skills and master new skills through trial and error without suffering the consequences of failure in real life. You can prepare for new events in your life or practice skills you wish to master, such as public speaking, acting, painting, or sports skills.

While Lucid Dreaming, you will improve your decision-making by giving you a chance to explore different possible outcomes so you can weigh the pros and cons and make the best choices for your life. This can also help you avoid making impulsive decisions that can cause problems in the future.

Enhance Your Emotional Intelligence

Become more self-aware and understand your emotional response to situations. By interpreting your subconscious thoughts and feelings in your dreams, you can practice being more self-aware in life. Being more self-aware can help you be more emotionally intelligent and better at managing emotions in stressful situations.

You can practice compassion for yourself and others and develop healthy relationships in your waking life. By being compassionate in your waking life, you can improve interactions

19

with others and make wiser choices to interact with others in your life positively. You can also become more empathetic towards others by understanding their feelings and motivations in their dreams.

You can also use lucid dreaming tools to help you deal with difficult emotions like anger or frustration in your daily life. By practicing your feelings in your sleep, you can learn how to control these emotions in stressful situations and adopt healthier ways of dealing with negative emotions in your daily life and your relationship.

Learning how to identify feelings in your dreams can help you learn how to control your emotional responses to situations in your waking life. You can learn to quickly identify the emotions you are feeling in your daily life and respond more mindfully to situations and people around you.

Your dream self is your subconscious or unconscious mind, and you can learn a lot about your waking self by exploring your subconscious in your dreams. By gaining control of your subconscious in dreams, you can learn to overcome obstacles in your waking life by increasing self-awareness and practicing various skills to use in your daily life.

By learning more about your subconscious in your dreams, you can improve your emotional intelligence in your daily life. You can also increase your ability to find creative solutions to everyday problems or develop novel ideas for your work or personal life. You will become more self-aware and understand your emotional responses to situations in your waking life so that you can relate better to yourself and others around you.

You can learn how to encourage others or tell them what's bothering you in a way that doesn't cause conflict or hurt feelings. By learning how to be more emotionally intelligent in your waking life, you can better manage your emotions in real life and respond more mindfully to situations and people around you.

You will gain greater insight into other people's motives and states of mind. You will start understanding others' feelings and motivations so you can build healthier and more authentic relationships with those around you.

Build emotional resilience by providing a safe space to experiment with different emotions and test new responses in dreams before you try them in real life. You can practice different responses in dreams to difficult emotions such as frustration or anger to respond more mindfully to situations in your real life.

Heal Yourself from Trauma and Anxiety

Lucidity provides the distance from which traumas may be re-experienced and reprocessed, so it is possible to come to new and deeper realizations about them. Lucid dreams may be an important therapeutic tool in assisting individuals in working through unresolved traumas, releasing them from their unconscious grip.

Lucid dreaming can help survivors of traumatic events heal by enabling them to re-experience the traumatic event in a dream state. Being able to process trauma without being overwhelmed by emotional arousal can help you overcome trauma more healthily and learn from the experience to make better choices in the future.

Lucid dreaming can also alleviate anxiety by helping you project yourself to places you feel the most anxious and in control. This can help you feel more relaxed in stressful situations and lower stress levels so you can deal more effectively with anxiety and fear in your waking life. Working through anxiety and fear in dreams helps you become more resilient to anxiety in your waking life and cope with it more effectively.

Lucid dreaming can also alleviate panic attacks by helping you learn to control your fear and anxiety in stressful situations through conscious choice. By learning to control fear in dreams, you can effectively equip yourself to handle fear in your waking life.

Nightmares no longer have power over the dreamer because it becomes possible to dissociate from them and accept them as just meaningless remnants from non-lucid, non-conscious states.

Practicing healthy coping mechanisms within the dream state may lead to their usage during waking life, and lucid dreaming has been shown to positively affect anti-anxiety therapy and medication use.

Overcome Your Fears

By facing your fears in a safe and controlled environment, you can also learn to control them in your life. By overcoming your dreams, you can develop the mindset to overcome fears in your waking life.

Lucid dreams help you face your fears by showing you what frightens you so you can learn to control your fear in real life. By facing your fears in dreams, you can practice techniques to help you overcome fear in your waking life.

You can understand the root of your fears to work on overcoming them in real life. By understanding your fears in dreams, you can become more aware of them in your waking life and learn how to overcome them effectively in the future.

Lucid nightmares, or nightmares derived from lucid dreams, can help understand real-life fears or phobias. Nightmares derived from lucid dreams can be very disturbing to the dreamer and may be hard to deal with. Nightmares derived from lucid dreams can help individuals understand their fears and phobias and learn how to reduce their anxiety in everyday life.

Practicing coping mechanisms and desensitizing yourself to your true fears is a great benefit. You manage to build confidence by conquering your fears in dreams. This can help you build your self-esteem and learn to believe in yourself.

Improve Your Physical Health

Lucid dreaming can be used as a form of self-hypnosis to improve physical health and relieve chronic pain. By practicing positive affirmations and visualizations in dreams, you can increase your threshold for pain and resilience to pain in life.

Lucid dreaming may act as an effective tool for pain management through its ability to extinguish pain signals. Lucid dreaming may help alleviate pain by helping you control pain signals and develop new coping mechanisms to limit the severity of physical pain in your waking life.

Rehearse healthy behaviors and make positive changes to your routine to improve your physical and mental health. Mental health interventions have been shown to improve physical health outcomes. By practicing positive behaviors in dreams, you can increase your physical resilience and adopt new habits. You can reduce stress and anxiety, which leads to improved physical health. By reducing your stress and dealing with anxiety in your dreams, you can reduce your anxiety.

Lucid dreaming helps you boost your immune system and improve your healing process by allowing you to access your subconscious mind and experience things from a more objective perspective. This can help you make decisions based on fact rather than intuition and emotion, which can often be clouded by fear or stress.

Connect with Your Spirituality

Have you ever wished you could talk to a loved one who passed away? Or wanted to ask God for guidance on a difficult decision? While we can't always get the answers we're looking for in life; spirituality is often more accessible through lucid dreaming.

We'll look at some of the ways that people have used lucid dreaming throughout history and learn about some of its benefits. Whether you consider yourself spiritual or not, there are many reasons why connecting with your spirituality through lucid dreaming might be beneficial for you.

What Is Spirituality?

Spirituality means different things to different people. For some, it may simply refer to a belief in something greater than ourselves, while others may see it as a way to connect with their culture or community. There is no right or wrong answer regarding what spirituality means - it is entirely personal. However, if you would like to explore your spirituality further, then using lucidity could be a helpful tool.

There are many ways in which spiritually-oriented individuals have used lucid dreams throughout history - from communicating with deceased loved ones, known as dream incubation, to seeking guidance from deities, known as divine Lucid Dreaming. Some people also use Lucid Dreaming practices for energy healing purposes - for themselves or others, known as energetic Lucid Dreaming. No matter what your beliefs are, there are likely ways in which connecting with your spirituality through dreaming could be beneficial for you.

How Can Lucid Dreaming Help You Connect with Your Spirituality?

There are many ways in which lucid dreaming can help you connect with your spirituality. Here are some of the most common:

Divine Lucid Dreaming: This is the practice of using lucidity to communicate with deities or other spiritual beings. If you have a specific question that you would like guidance on, this could be a helpful way to get answers. It's also a great way to build a stronger relationship with your chosen deity.

Dream Incubation: The practice of using lucidity to communicate with deceased loved ones. If you have someone in your life that you miss and would like to talk to them again, this could be a way to do so. It can also help get closure on unresolved issues.

Energetic Lucid Dreaming: This is the practice of using lucid dreaming for energy healing - for yourself or others. This could be a great option if you are looking for a way to connect with your spirituality through healing. Many different techniques fall under this category, so there is likely something that will work well for you no matter what your beliefs are.

No matter what your spiritual beliefs are, there are likely ways in which connecting with your spirituality through lucid dreaming could be beneficial for you. Whether you want to communicate with deities or other spiritual beings, seek guidance from those who have passed away, or use energy healing practices - there are many options available to explore. Take some time to experiment and find what works best for you.

Experience Lucid Living

Lucid dreaming has many benefits that can improve your life in various ways. One of the most unique and beneficial aspects of lucid dreaming is "lucid living". Lucid living is when you become aware that you are dreaming while still awake and conscious. This allows you to take control of your dream and change it into whatever you want or need it to be.

There are many benefits to being able to experience lucid living, such as being able to control your dreams, boost your creativity, problem-solve better, heal from trauma or anxiety, overcome fears, and even improve your physical health. In addition, lucid living can also enhance connecting with your spirituality and experiencing different cultures through travel.

One of the most beneficial aspects of lucid living is that you can take control of your dream. This means that if there is something in your life that you are struggling with, you can use your dreams to work through those issues. You can also use lucid dreaming to boost your creativity by using it as a space to explore new ideas and possibilities.

Lucid living can also be used as a therapy for trauma or anxiety. By facing your fears in a controlled environment, such as a dream, you can begin to heal and work through any issues causing these problems. In addition, overcoming fears, in general, can be made easier by practicing in a safe space like this. Improving physical health is another benefit of lucid living – working on visualization and positive thinking. At the same time, awake and conscious, people have been able to make significant improvements in their physical well-being by changing their mindset alone!

In conclusion, many benefits are associated with being able to experience Lucid Living. These include having control over your dream, improving creativity, problem-solving, overcoming fears, healing from trauma or anxiety, and improving physical health.

Chapter 3: Risks of Lucid Dreaming

Sleep Paralysis

Sleep paralysis is a condition that can occur either during falling asleep or waking up. It is characterized by the inability to move or speak and may be accompanied by hallucinations. Sleep paralysis can be a frightening experience, but it is not dangerous and usually lasts only a few minutes. However, it can be recurring, and some people may experience it regularly. Several possible causes of sleep paralysis include sleeping in an uncomfortable position, stress, anxiety, lack of sleep, and certain medications. Treatment typically involves managing conditions such as anxiety or stress and practicing good sleep hygiene.

There are two types of sleep paralysis: isolated sleep paralysis and recurrent isolated sleep paralysis. Isolated sleep paralysis is a one-time event not associated with any other condition. Recurrent isolated sleep paralysis, on the other hand, is when a person experiences multiple episodes of sleep paralysis over time. While sleep paralysis can be a frightening experience, it is not dangerous and usually only lasts for a few minutes.

Sleep Paralysis Symptoms:

The main symptom of sleep paralysis is the inability to move or speak while falling asleep or waking up. This can be accompanied by:
- Hallucinations: Seeing, hearing, or feeling things that are not there
- Sensations of being paralyzed

- Shortness of breath
- Chest pain
- Heart palpitations

Sleep paralysis typically lasts for a few minutes but can feel much longer. In some cases, it may last for several hours. Sleep paralysis is often recurrent, meaning people may experience multiple episodes over time. It can happen at any age but is most common in young adults and adolescents.

Causes of Sleep Paralysis:

Several possible causes of sleep paralysis include sleeping in an uncomfortable position, stress, anxiety, lack of sleep, and certain medications. It is also more common in people with narcolepsy or other sleep disorders.

Risk Factors for Sleep Paralysis:

Some factors that may increase your risk of experiencing sleep paralysis include:
- Depression
- Bipolar disorder
- Anxiety disorders
- Post-traumatic stress disorder (PTSD)

Sleep paralysis can be a frightening experience, but it is not dangerous. It usually lasts only a few minutes, but it can feel much longer.

False Awakenings

False awakenings are a type of lucid dream where the individual believes they have awoken from their sleep when they are still dreaming. False awakenings can be extremely realistic and often occur after another lucidity-inducing event such as sleep paralysis or hypnagogia. While false awakenings can be benign, for some individuals, these experiences can lead to feelings of anxiety and confusion. It is important to remember that if you suspect you have a false awakening, perform a reality check to determine whether you are truly awake or still dreaming.

There are three main types of false awakenings:

1. Waking up in your normal bed, Type 1: If you are dreaming and you are in your normal bed, you are likely dreaming. You may feel awake, but you are not because you are still dreaming.
2. Waking up in an unusual location, Type 2: In this type of false awakening, you suddenly find yourself in a completely different space from your bed or your usual location.
3. Multiple false awakenings, Type 3: These false awakenings often occur after other types of lucid dreaming, such as sleep paralysis or hypnagogia. They occur most often in individuals with a predisposition to lucid dreaming, though anyone can experience this type of false awakening.

Type 1 is considered the most common and least distressing type of false awakening, while Type 3 is considered the rarest but most distressful type. Although it may be difficult to tell the difference between a regular dream and a false awakening at first, certain signs may help clues you into the fact that you're not awake. For example, in a false awakening, you may find that your dream environment is too perfect or that you have superhuman abilities. Alternatively, reality should feel "off" in some way – such as colors being brighter than usual or objects appearing out of place.

If you think you might be experiencing a false awakening, there are certain things you can do to perform a reality check and determine whether you are dreaming or not. For example, like two-headed animals, try to fly or look for impossible objects. In addition, try reading something close up and then looking away – in dreams, the text often changes when viewed from afar. Finally, electrical appliances such as phones or light switches may not work properly in dreams, so checking to see if they function normally can also help clue you in on the fact that you're still asleep.

While false awakenings can be confusing and sometimes anxiety-inducing experiences, it is important to remember that they are harmless and relatively common within the lucid dreaming community. If you suspect you have a false awakening, simply performing a reality check should help ease any fears and allow you to enjoy the experience!

Sleep Deprivation

Sleep deprivation has many risks, including mental health problems, anxiety, depression, and isolation. Sleep deprivation can also lead to hallucinations and delusions.

Some of the most common mental health risks associated with sleep deprivation include:

Anxiety: Research suggests that sleep deprivation can increase anxiety levels and cause anxiety-related disorders to develop over time. In addition, decreased sleep quality can also cause anxiety disorders to flare up and cause panic attacks in individuals prone to these episodes.

Depression: Many people report feeling depressed after not getting adequate sleep. Insomnia can lead to feelings of isolation, and decreased social connections can make it more difficult to treat depression.

Schizophrenia: Sleep deprivation can cause hallucinations and delusions in some people. In these situations, sleep deprivation can directly cause the symptoms of schizophrenia to flare up and worsen. However, research has also suggested that sleep deprivation can contribute to the development of schizophrenia in vulnerable people due to family history or genetics.

Suicidal Ideation: Research has shown that sleep deprivation can increase the risk of suicidal thoughts and behaviors. In addition, some research has suggested that sleep deprivation can cause a person to become more susceptible to suicidal thinking if they have a predisposition to mental illness or suicidal thoughts.

Mental health problems: Sleep deprivation is a major risk factor for developing mental health problems such as anxiety and depression. It can also worsen existing mental health conditions.

Isolation: Chronically sleep-deprived People often isolate themselves from others because they don't have the energy to socialize. This can lead to feelings of loneliness and isolation.

Hallucinations: People who are chronically sleep-deprived often experience hallucinations. This means they see, hear, or feel things that are not there. Hallucinations can be frightening and confusing.

Delusions: Chronically sleep-deprived People often experience delusions. This means that they believe things that are not true. Delusions can be dangerous because they can lead to risky behavior.

Unwanted nightmares

It is not uncommon to have nightmares while lucid dreaming. Many people find that they are more prone to having nightmares when they know they are dreaming. This can be particularly distressing for those who suffer from anxiety or other mental health conditions. Unwanted nightmares often occur after experiencing a particularly frightening or traumatic dream. If you have experienced such a dream while lucid, consider waiting until you wake up to avoid having it again while lucid. Sometimes, however, unwanted nightmares can occur if the dreamer is nervous about becoming lucid or trying to recall a previous dream. To prevent unwanted nightmares from occurring, try to relax and avoid thinking about becoming lucid or trying to recall past dreams before going to sleep.

Nightmares can also occur after experiencing a particularly strange or traumatic dream or waking up from a dream involving something traumatic or frightening. Often, these dreams are caused by powerful emotions being stirred up during sleep and can be difficult to forget while awake. However, focusing on pleasant things and practicing mindfulness can be useful in reducing the intensity and frequency of unwanted nightmares.

Nightmares are common within the general population and the lucid dreaming community. Sometimes, nightmares can cause psychological distress – particularly if they become a recurring issue or involve something frightening or traumatic. Suppose you're struggling with unwanted nightmares while lucid dreaming; it's important to seek professional help so that they can help you get the help that you need.

While it is unclear why some people are more likely to have nightmares during a lucid dream, there are a few possible explanations. One theory is that the increased awareness of being in a dream state may cause the mind to become overstimulated, leading to disturbing or frightening images appearing in the dreamscape. Another possibility is that individuals with anxiety or other mental health conditions may be more susceptible to having negative dreams due to their heightened sense of worry and stress.

Some ways to reduce the chances of having an unwanted nightmare include avoiding Lucid Dreaming when feeling anxious or stressed, setting intentions for positive dreams before falling asleep, and keeping a journal nearby so you can record any negative dreams immediately upon waking up. If you experience a nightmare while Lucid Dreaming, try your best not to wake yourself up completely – instead, focus on changing the scene around you into something more pleasant.

Unwanted nightmares are a natural part of lucid dreaming. However, they can cause psychological distress and distress if waking yourself up results in the dream continuing.

Although Lucid Dreaming comes with several risks, it is still an incredibly fascinating and useful tool that can be used for personal growth and exploration. With proper precautions in place, many risks can be mitigated, allowing you to experience the full benefits of this unique state of consciousness.

Waking Life Confusion

It's not uncommon to feel disoriented after waking up from a dream. But for some people, this confusion can last all day long and make it hard to function in day-to-day life. This is known as waking life confusion, one of the risks associated with lucid dreaming. Waking life confusion can happen anytime you wake up from a dream, but it's not necessarily associated with lucid dreaming itself. It can have some causes, such as sleep deprivation and drinking alcohol before bed. If you frequently feel disoriented upon waking, try to adjust your diet and lifestyle so that you get more restful sleep and consume less alcohol before bed. In addition, it's important to note that people with mental illnesses such as schizophrenia may experience greater waking life confusion than individuals without mental illness.

Waking life confusion can be dangerous for people who suffer from a mental illness such as schizophrenia because confusion can significantly exacerbate symptoms and worsen their condition. Symptoms of schizophrenia include hallucinations, delusions, and disorganized thoughts – all of which are often accompanied by a feeling of disorientation and confusion in the waking world. Therefore, it's important to seek medical assistance and treatment if you notice symptoms of schizophrenia worsening or if your waking life confusion appears to become more severe.

Waking life confusion may also impact your ability to function in everyday life. Suppose you're feeling confused about what is happening around you and find it difficult to interact with people in normal circumstances. In that case, you may experience problems at school or work, leading to social isolation and feelings of isolation or loneliness. Suppose you're living with schizophrenia or other mental illness and experiencing waking life confusion. In that case, it's important to seek help from a doctor or therapist to get the treatment you need and find a way to manage your symptoms effectively.

Waking life confusion happens when people have trouble separating their dreams from reality. This can lead to them feeling confused and disoriented all day long. The problem is that when you're in a state of wakefulness, your brain is supposed to be processing information from the outside world, not dreams. So when you're constantly trying to reconcile two different sets of information, it takes a toll on your mental health.

Symptoms of waking life confusion include:

• Feeling disoriented or confused all day long
• Having trouble separating your dreams from reality
• Feeling like you're in a dream even when you're awake
• Hallucinating (seeing, hearing, or smelling things that aren't there)

- Feeling like you're floating or that the ground isn't under your feet
- Feeling depressed, anxious, or overstimulated

Increased Anxiety

Many people worry that lucid dreaming will increase their anxiety levels. While it is true that some people may experience increased anxiety while lucid dreaming, there are ways to prevent or manage this side effect.

While it is possible to experience increased anxiety while lucid dreaming, several things you can do to prevent or manage this side effect; first, try to relax and focus on your breathing when you become aware that you are dreaming. Second, if you start to feel anxious or panicked during a dream, remind yourself that it is only a dream and cannot hurt you. Third, practice visualization exercises before bedtime to calm your mind and body before going to sleep. Finally, if lucidity triggers feelings of anxiety or panic, consider seeking professional help from a therapist or counselor who specializes in treating anxiety disorders.

While it is natural to experience some anxiety while dreaming or while simply thinking about lucid dreaming, it is important to seek help if you experience persistent feelings of worry or anxiety while lucid or thinking about lucid dreaming. In most cases, increased anxiety after lucid dreaming is only temporary and should subside once the dream is over.

Anxiety Disorders:

Generalized Anxiety Disorder (GAD): People with GAD worry excessively about everyday things that others would not normally consider stressful. They may have trouble sleeping, feeling tense or on edge, and have difficulty concentrating.

Panic Disorder: Panic disorder is characterized by recurrent panic attacks, which are sudden periods of intense fear or discomfort that peak within minutes. Physical symptoms include heart palpitations, shortness of breath, and dizziness. People with panic disorder often live in fear of having another attack and may avoid places or situations where they think an attack could happen.

Social Anxiety Disorder: Also known as social phobia, social anxiety disorder is a type of anxiety disorder that involves intense feelings of self-consciousness and embarrassment in social situations. People with a social anxiety disorder may avoid public speaking or other activities where others could judge them.
Obsessive-Compulsive Disorder (OCD): OCD is an anxiety disorder characterized by obsessions and compulsions.

How to prevent or manage increased anxiety while lucid dreaming

To help manage anxiety while lucid dreaming, it's important to take a step back and remind yourself that it is only a dream and cannot hurt you. Then focus on breathing and try relaxation techniques to calm your mind and body. Finally, remember that anxiety only lasts a few minutes and will eventually fade away if you stay calm and remind yourself that it is only a dream. If anxiety persists or if you need additional help managing feelings of anxiety or panic while lucid dreaming, visit your doctor or mental health professional for diagnosis. In some cases, medications or therapy can effectively manage anxiety while lucid dreaming and allow you to continue enjoying the benefits of lucid dreaming.

The main steps to prevent or manage increased anxiety are:

-Relax and focus on your breathing when you become aware that you are dreaming.
-If you start to feel anxious or panicked during a dream, remind yourself that it is only a dream and cannot hurt you.
-Practice visualization exercises before bedtime to calm your mind and body before going to sleep.
-If lucidity triggers feelings of anxiety or panic, consider seeking professional help from a therapist or counselor who specializes in treating anxiety disorders.

Isolation and hallucinations

Isolation and hallucinations are two of the risks associated with lucid dreaming. Lucid dreaming can be a very isolating experience, as it can be difficult to share dreams with others. Additionally, some people may find that their lucid dreams become more frequent or intense when they are isolated from other people. Hallucinations are another potential risk of lucidity, as some people may see things not really there during a dream.

There are several reasons for isolation and hallucinations during a lucid dream:

1. Isolation can occur if you cannot connect with the people around you in the physical world because of

your hallucinations or confusion during the waking state.
2.   Isolation might occur if you cannot communicate with others outside of lucid dreams because that is how they choose to leave their connections in your waking world.
3.   Isolation can occur if you fear sharing your lucid dreams with others or that others will not believe your experiences are real or valid.
4.

Isolation and hallucinations can be another difficult side effect of lucid dreaming to face. However, suppose you cannot connect with other people due to isolation or hallucinations during a dream. In that case, exploring these reasons with an open mind is important to find solutions that can help you reconnect with people in both your waking and dreaming worlds. You may need to reevaluate how you are interacting with others in your waking world and ask yourself if this is a healthy way to stay connected with others in your waking life.

Some people may find that they have more success with lucid dreaming when they are isolated from others. This is because they can focus more on their internal thoughts and experiences without distractions from the outside world. Additionally, isolation can increase feelings of loneliness and anxiety, making it easier to have a lucidity trigger happen during a dream.

People who suffer from sleep paralysis often report hallucinations, which could be because they are unable to move or speak while in this state. This can lead to them seeing things that are not there, feeling like someone is watching them, or trying to hurt them even though no one is present. This feeling of isolation can lead to a greater chance of having a lucid dream as the brain begins to believe that the person is indeed alone, and hallucinations begin to take over their senses. This is not considered a mental disorder but rather a temporary occurrence during sleep paralysis that the brain has trouble processing due to being awake while the body is still asleep. This sleep paralysis often happens when you wake up in the middle of the night and cannot move. Many people suffering from this sleep disorder will also frequently suffer from lucid dreams.

Chapter 4: Get Ready for Lucid Dreaming

Sleep Habits and Dreams

Sleep is a vital part of our lives and has a profound impact on our health and well-being. Most people need around eight hours of sleep per night, although some people may need more or less. The quality of our sleep is just as important as the quantity.

In order to have successful lucid dreams, it is important to have good sleeping habits. This means going to bed at roughly the same time every night and getting enough hours of sleep. It also means creating an environment that promotes relaxation and comfort such as keeping the room dark and quiet and avoiding electronics before bedtime.

Once you have good sleeping habits, you can start experimenting with different techniques for inducing lucidity. Some people find that certain supplements such as galantamine or B6 can be helpful in inducing lucidity. Others find that listening to binaural beats or using specialized light-emitting glasses helps them achieve lucidity more easily. There is no one "right" way to induce lucidity; it really depends on what works best for you personally.

This chapter will cover some basic information about sleep and dreams as well as ways to increase your chances of having a lucid dream

The Four Stages of Sleep

Sleep is a naturally occurring state of rest for the mind and body. It is characterized by changes in brain activity, heart rate, and breathing. There are four stages of sleep: rapid eye movement (REM) sleep, light sleep (N1), deeper sleep (N2), and deep sleep (N3).

During REM sleep, your brain activity increases, and your eyes move rapidly from side to side. Dreaming is possible during other stages of sleep, but when you awaken from REM sleep, you are more likely to remember being fully immersed in a vivid, narrative-driven experience.

REM periods begin short and gradually lengthen toward early morning. Light Sleep (N1) is known as "light" or "transitional" sleep because it occurs as you transition from awake to asleep. This is the stage at which you gradually lose awareness of your surroundings and bodily functions such as breathing and heart rate begin to slow.

Deeper sleep (N2) is a stage of light sleep from which it is difficult to wake up. During this stage, your brain waves slow down and become smaller. Deep sleep (N3) occurs primarily in the early hours of the night, with little to no deep sleep occurring in the latter half of your nightly sleep session.

During this stage, your muscles become paralyzed because your brain prevents electrical and chemical signals from reaching your body, a condition known as sleep paralysis. Sleep paralysis can be accompanied by hallucinations, which can be either pleasant or terrifying. The paralysis usually lasts only a few minutes, but it can feel much longer.

Some people experience hypnagogic hallucinations during N1 or N2 sleep. These hallucinations can take many forms, such as hearing voices or seeing images that are not really there. Hypnagogic hallucinations are generally brief and occur just before falling asleep or upon waking from sleep.

Night terrors are another type of hallucination that can occur during deep sleep (N3). Night terrors are characterized by a feeling of terror or panic that wakes you up from sleep abruptly. Unlike nightmares, night terrors are not usually recalled after waking up; however, they can leave you feeling shaken and frightened.

Sleepwalking, or somnambulism, is a parasomnia that occurs during N3 sleep. Sleepwalkers often do not remember their episodes, although they may have some fragmentary memories. Episodes typically last for less than 30 minutes, but they can occasionally last for an hour or more. During an episode, a person may get out of bed and walk around, perform complex tasks, or engage in behaviors that are out of character. In severe cases, people have been known to drive cars or even cook meals while asleep.

Sleep talking, or somniloquy, is another parasomnia that can occur during any stage of sleep. It is characterized by talking aloud while asleep without being aware of it. Sleep talking can range from simple muttering to complex conversations. It usually lasts for less than 30 seconds, but it can occasionally go on for several minutes.

Both somnambulism and somniloquy tend to run in families and are more common in children than adults. They are also more common in people with certain mental disorders, such as schizophrenia.

Sleep paralysis is a condition that can occur during any stage of sleep; however, it is most common during REM sleep. Sleep paralysis is characterized by a feeling of being paralyzed or unable to move. This paralysis can last for a few seconds to a few minutes. Some people also experience hallucinations during sleep paralysis, which can be either pleasant or terrifying. Sleep paralysis is generally harmless and does not cause any long-term effects; however, it can be quite frightening for those who experience it.

Maintain Positive Sleep Habits

A lot of people don't realize how important sleep is for our overall health and well-being. Getting a good night's sleep can help improve our mood, memory, and focus. It can also help reduce stress and anxiety. Not to mention, it can also help us dream more and recognize that we're dreaming more.

One of the best things you can do for your sleep is to practice good sleep hygiene. This means creating habits that promote restful sleep and avoiding habits that disrupt sleep. Some tips for good sleep hygiene include:

Control light exposure: Every day, get some bright, early-morning sunlight. This helps to regulate your body's natural circadian rhythm. At night, dim the lights in your home and avoid looking at screens for at least 30 to 60 minutes before going to bed.

Turn off electronics: Electronics emit blue light, which can suppress melatonin production and make it harder to fall asleep. Avoid using electronic devices—including TVs, laptops, smartphones, and tablets—in the hours leading up to bedtime.

Late-night caffeine and alcohol: Caffeine is a stimulant that can stay in your system for six hours or more. Alcohol may make you feel drowsy at first, but it can actually disrupt your sleep later in the night. Avoid caffeine and alcohol in the evening or late at night.

Only use your bed for sleep or intimacy: Your bed should be associated with sleep and relaxation. If you work from home or spend a lot of time in bed during the day, try to create a separate space for work or other activities. This will help train your brain to associate your bed with sleep.

Relax before going to bed: Do something relaxing in the hour before you go to bed—such as reading or taking a bath—to help transition from wakefulness to sleepiness.

Avoid planning, worrying about the future, or reflecting on the past: These activities can increase anxiety and make it harder to fall asleep. Instead, concentrate on feeling good about what you accomplished during the day.

Look forward to realizing your dreams: Be curious and eager to see what your dreaming mind has to show you as you lie in bed. As you prepare to sleep, be aware that you will soon have several opportunities to become lucid and remember your dreams.

By following these tips, you can create healthy sleep habits that will help you get the restful sleep you need.

Sleep Hygiene

Keep Healthy Sleep Habits

Healthy sleep habits will give you more opportunities to dream and recognize that you're dreaming. When well-rested, your mind is clearer and capable of exploring new ideas. This enables you to have richer, more meaningful dreams. When you're tired, your thoughts are muddled, and your attention is scattered. You may not be able to focus on anything for very long, making it difficult to get deep into the creative process or remember your dreams. In addition, when you don't get enough sleep, your body doesn't function as well as it should. This can lead to weight gain, increased stress, and difficulty concentrating. Get adequate sleep every night to get the most out of your dreams and improve your overall health. A few things can help make this easier: avoid caffeine in the morning, avoid working or studying in bed, keep a regular sleep schedule, and limit exposure to light in the hours before bedtime.

Waking from dreams in the night can help you practice induction techniques. One of the best ways to become lucid is to train your mind to recognize when you're dreaming. You can do this by keeping a dream journal and recording your dreams every morning or practicing reality checks throughout the day. Reality checking is simply asking yourself whether you're awake or dreaming. If you're dreaming, you'll usually find things are not quite as they should be. For example, you might be able to fly or walk through walls. If you're having trouble doing reality checks during the day, try setting an alarm for a few hours before your usual bedtime and waking yourself up intentionally. Then, do a reality check and try to fall back asleep immediately. You may find that this increases your chances of becoming lucid at night.

Keep a good Sleep Hygiene.

Just as there are certain things you can do to promote physical health, there are also specific things you can do to encourage healthy sleep habits. This is called sleep hygiene. Some basic sleep hygiene practices include: maintaining a regular sleep schedule; avoiding caffeine and alcohol before bed; reserving the bed for sleep and intimacy; winding down before sleep with relaxation techniques; and quieting the mind as you fall asleep by focusing on relaxing your muscles or imagining a peaceful nature scene. Following these simple guidelines, you can train your body and mind to associate the bed with sleep and reduce the likelihood of restless nights.

Practice Relaxation: Relaxation techniques such as deep breathing exercises or progressive muscle relaxation can help reduce stress and promote healthy sleep habits. To practice deep breathing, inhale slowly through your nose while counting to four, then exhale slowly through your mouth while counting to four. Repeat this process until you feel yourself beginning to relax. For progressive muscle relaxation, start by tensing all the muscles in your feet for five seconds, then releasing them completely and allowing them to relax for 30 seconds. Move up through each muscle group in your body until you reach your head/neck area; then reverse the order back down until you reach your feet again.

Avoid caffeine and alcohol late in the day: Caffeine is a stimulant that can keep you awake and make it difficult to fall asleep. For this reason, it's best to avoid caffeine in the afternoon and evening hours. Alcohol, on the other hand, may make you drowsy at first, but it disrupts sleep later in the night. This is because alcohol prevents you from reaching the deepest stages of sleep, which are important for feeling rested when you wake up. If you're struggling to sleep through the night, avoid drinking alcohol in the evening and limit your intake of caffeinated beverages during the day.

Regulate light exposure: The human body has an internal clock that regulates many functions based on the cycles of light and darkness. This clock is known as the circadian rhythm. When it's dark outside, our bodies produce melatonin, a hormone that makes us feel sleepy. In contrast, when it's light out, our bodies stop producing melatonin, and we feel more alert. This natural process makes regulating our exposure to light important to maintaining healthy sleep habits. During the daytime, get plenty of natural sunlight (or artificial bright light exposure if you work night shifts). In the evening, avoid screen time for at least an hour before bedtime and dim the lights in your home to signal to your body that it's time to start producing melatonin again.

Wind down before sleep: It's important to give yourself time to wind down before bed so that your mind and body are relaxed when you finally lie down. You can wind down several ways before sleep, such as reading a book, taking a bath, or writing in a journal. Find what works best for you and stick to a routine so that your body knows it's time to prepare for slumber when you start your winding-down activities.

Recalling Your Dreams

To lucid dream more frequently, you must remember your dreams. While in the sleep state, many people are likely to have dreams. When you wake up from your dreams, it is important to remember what you just experienced. Many people use a "recall strategy" where they set a goal for themselves to remember their dreams and then wake up and attempt to recall them. It is also important to focus on the visuals while dreaming and not get lost in thought. Lucid dreaming usually occurs when an individual recalls specific, vivid images during their dream state. When you awaken from your sleep, it is an opportune time to recollect your dreams as you are still relatively awake. When people awaken in the middle of the night, they have trouble recalling their dreams due to REM (rapid eye movement) sleep taking over at that time. If this is the case for you, try jogging your mind by recalling common dream categories such as emotions, settings, colors, or actions.

Remembering your dreams is not easy at first, but with practice, it becomes easier. When starting, make a list of ten goals that are related to lucid dreaming and review them every day before bed. Also, keep a journal where you can record all of your dreams upon waking up so that you do not forget any of them. Finally, if you find yourself struggling with recall, often set the alarm for four and a half or six hours after turning off the lights so that it will remind you to start dreaming again during the REM sleep phase.

To be able to lucid dream more frequently, one must remember their dreams as soon as they wake up from them. Many times when someone wakes up in the middle of the night, they have trouble recalling their Dreams because REM Sleep takes over at that time; however, there are ways around this problem by using strategies such as Jogging Your Mind or setting an alarm clock for four and a half or six hours after turning off lights to help remind yourself about Dreams during this stage of sleep.

One way to try and remember your dreams is by setting a goal for yourself to remember them and then attempt to recall what happened in your dream once you wake up. It is also important to focus on the visuals while dreaming and not get lost in thought because Lucid dreaming usually occurs when an individual recalls specific, vivid images during their dream state. If you find that you are struggling with recalling your dreams often, set the alarm for four and a half or six hours after turning off the lights so that it will remind you to start dreaming again during the REM sleep phase.

Many ways can help you remember your dreams, such as keeping a journal, setting goals related to lucid dreaming, or reviewing common dream categories. Paying attention to nocturnal awakenings can also help increase your ability to recall dreams and set an alarm clock for four and a half or six hours after turning off lights. Although remembering your dreams may be difficult at first, with practice, it will become easier over time.

Prepare for Dream Journaling

To develop high-level dream recall, you should begin journaling your dreams regularly. This will help you understand your dreams and their meanings better. You can learn how to use your dreams for guidance in your daily life by paying close attention to them. When you keep a dream journal, you can share your dreams with others. This is a fantastic way to broaden your understanding of the subconscious mind and form friendships based on common interests.

A dream journal can be kept in a variety of ways. You can keep a notebook, an online journal, or even record your dreams on audio or video. Finding a method that works for you and can stick with over time is critical. The more consistent you are, the better the results.

1. Determine which method works best for you. If you're not comfortable writing in a journal, find an alternative method that works for you.

2. Make time each night to write down your dreams. This will help you remember your dreams better over time.

3. Be aware of your surroundings while dreaming and take notes on what is happening around you. This will assist you in better understanding the symbolism of your dreams.

4. Pay close attention to details in your dreams and write them down as precisely as possible. This can assist you in better understanding your dreams and their meaning.

5. Be patient; your dream journal may take some time to produce results. The more consistent you are, however, the better your chances of improving your dream recall and

developing meaningful friendships based on shared interests in your dreams.

Keep within easy access: To get started, keep the journal within **easy access**. This might be on your nightstand or next to your bed. Keeping it nearby will help you track your dreams and make connections between them.

Write down everything: Do not censor yourself; write everything that comes to mind in your dream journal. This will help you to understand your dreams and their meaning better.

Keywords: When you first wake up in the morning, before leaving the bed, take a few moments to write down the main keywords from your dream. These will be key points you'll want to remember when you write out your full dream report.

Date: When you're ready to record your dreams, set a **date** for each entry. This will help you record your progress and track the changes that occur over time.

Title: Give each dream a **title** that represents the main theme. For example, if you dream about flying, you might title the dream "Taking Flight." This will help you better understand your dream's content and make connections between it and other dreams.

Summary: Next, write a summary of the main points of your dream. This will provide a quick overview of what happened in the dream and how it relates to your life. Try to be concise while providing enough detail to help you remember the dream.

Characters: Next, list all the characters in your dream. Did you recognize anyone? If so, how did they make you feel? How did they contribute to the dream's overall meaning?

Themes: Finally, identify common themes or motifs in your dreams. Add any relevant insights that you may have about the content of the dream.

Events: Describe any specific events in your dream, including what happened and who was involved. Be sure to include any significant symbolism or hidden messages relevant to you.

Settings: Describe the setting of your dream, including where you were and what kind of environment you were in. Remember to include any significant details that will help you to understand the dream better.

Objects: Did any objects appear in your dream? If so, what were they and what did they symbolize? What was your dream's overall message?

Emotions: Once you have a title, begin creating your dream report by **describing the emotions** you felt during the dream. Were you scared? Excited? Anxious? Confused? Then, express your thoughts and beliefs about what the dream may mean. What do you think it represents in your life? What could it be trying to tell you?

Actions: Finally, list all the actions that occurred in your dream. What were you doing? Who was with you? What did they do? Were any objects or people involved in these actions?

Dream Analysis: Now that you have summarized the main points of your dream, it is time to analyze it further. Try to identify recurring themes or motifs throughout the dream, and explore what they might mean for you.

Interpretation: Lastly, reflect on any changes you've noticed in yourself since having the dream. Have you been more open to taking risks? Have you been feeling more confident? How did the emotions in the dream affect you? What do you think the dream's symbolism is trying to tell you? Write out your thoughts and reflections in a cohesive and organized manner.

Share your journal with someone else: If you want to share it with someone else, be sure to do it safely and respectfully. Explain the journal's purpose and ask if they would like to participate. You can share edited excerpts from your dreams for others to read. This will allow them access to the symbolism but protect your privacy.

As you continue journaling your dreams, pay close attention to emerging patterns. Do certain symbols or themes seem to recur often? If so, what do you think they represent in your life? The more time and effort you put into understanding your dreams, the more insight they will provide into your subconscious mind and conscious life path. Keeping a dream journal is a powerful tool for self-discovery and personal growth. Use it to unlock the mysteries of your innermost thoughts and feelings, and you will be amazed at what you learn about yourself.

Practice: Create your dream journal

The following is an example of how to create a dream journal. Remember to be creative and personalize it to fit your needs.
Date: April 8th
Title: The Eagle and the Snake
Keywords: Flying, Eagles, Snakes, Desert, Sun
Summary: I am flying high above a desert landscape on the back of an eagle. The sun is beating down on me, but I feel exhilarated

and free. Suddenly, I see a snake coiled up on a rock below. The eagle starts to dive down towards it, and I feel a mix of excitement and fear.

I wake up just before the eagle grabs the snake.

Themes: Freedom, Fear, Excitement

Events: Flying on the back of an eagle, seeing a snake coiled up on a rock

Symbols: Eagle - freedom, power, Snakes - fear, danger

Emotions: Excitement, fear. I feel exhilarated and free when I am flying on the eagle's back. But when I see the snake below, I start to feel afraid.

Interpretation: The eagle represents my higher self or spiritual side, while the snake symbolizes my lower self or shadow side. The sun could represent my life purpose, and the desert landscape could be a metaphor for my challenges in achieving it. Alternatively, this dream could be interpreted to suggest that I am currently out of balance, with my lower self (snake) dominating my thoughts and actions. To achieve harmony and inner peace, I must work on balancing my inner energies and emotions.

The dream tells me I need to focus on my spiritual side, which the eagle represents. I also need to be aware of the dangers lurking around me, which the snake symbolizes. I can achieve a sense of freedom and peace by working on restoring balance within myself. This will allow me to overcome any challenges that come my way with ease.

Set your Lucid dreaming goals

To make the most of your time in lucid dreams, set goals that include clear and specific tasks that you can carry out within the dream. This will help to ground you in the reality of the dream and to keep you focused on what's important. When you have a goal in mind, staying focused during a dream conversation or activity is easier. Remember: always remember where you are and what's happening in the dream, even if it feels like you're losing track of things. By setting goals and sticking to them, you'll be able to accomplish more in lucid dreams than if you were wandering around aimlessly.

Additionally, try to avoid setting too many goals at once; when your brain is overwhelmed with too much information, it will tend to forget everything else. Instead, break your goals down into smaller and more manageable pieces. Once again, this will help keep your focus laser-focused on what's important.

As you begin to set your goals, you might consider flying, which is possible when you deconstruct your waking assumptions. What's stopping you from flying in real life? Probably a combination of things: the fear of heights, the belief that it's impossible to fly, etc. But in a dream, all of those limitations are gone. You can explore what it would be like to soar through the air without any worries or concerns holding you back. If you've ever wanted to try skydiving or parasailing, lucid dreaming is the perfect opportunity to do so without any risk.

Another great way to get started is by learning about your dream body. This can be a bit tricky, as you'll need to be patient and keep an open mind when exploring your dreams. But once you learn some basics about your dream body, it will be much easier to interact with it lucidly. For example, if you're struggling to move around in your dream, try focusing on specific areas of your body (e.g., hands or feet) and sense what's happening there. This can help you understand how your body works in your dream and open up new possibilities for movement.

Another way to get started is by exploring your dreams with a friend. If you have someone you trust who's also interested in lucid dreaming, sharing your experiences and asking for their input can be helpful. This can help you both learn more about each other's dreams and develop new techniques for achieving lucidity together. Exploring the dream together can be a fun and rewarding experience, and it can help you develop a stronger connection to your dreaming self.

Of course, balancing your goal-setting with spontaneously exploring the lucid dream world is also important. Don't get so caught up in accomplishing specific tasks that you forget to enjoy yourself and have fun! After all, one of the best parts about lucid dreaming is that anything is possible; if you can think it, you can do it. So go ahead and explore your wildest dreams, literally. Try out different activities and see what happens; you might be surprised at how much fun you have when no rules or limitations are holding you back. Remember: don't try to change your reality too much, or you won't see much transformation. If you want to make significant changes in your life, starting small and working your way up is best. By taking baby steps and gradually building up momentum, you'll be more likely to achieve lasting results that stick with you even after you wake up from the dream. Approaching lucidity step by step is a great way to make gradual, sustainable changes in your life.

Setting your lucid dreaming goals tips:

One of the best ways to maximize your lucidity experience is by setting specific goals for yourself. This way, you'll be more likely to achieve results. Here are some tips for setting lucid dreaming goals:

1. Make your goals specific and measurable. When you know exactly what you're trying to accomplish, it's much easier to measure your progress and stay motivated.
2. Start small and work your way up. Don't try to make too many drastic changes all at once. Take things one step at a time and see how you feel after each success.

3. Be patient and persistent. It can take some time to achieve consistent results with lucid dreaming, so don't get discouraged if the process takes a little longer than you expected. Just keep trying, and eventually, you'll reach your goals!

4. Stay upbeat. Lucid dreaming is an amazing experience, but it's not easy to achieve, don't let any setbacks get you down. Keep your attitude positive and focus on the goal; you'll be well on your way to success.

5. Be prepared for obstacles. Success in lucid dreaming comes with some challenges – be prepared for them, and you'll be able to overcome them easily.

Finally, don't forget that practice makes perfect. The more you lucid dream, the better you'll get at it. So keep trying, and soon you'll be enjoying the best lucid dreams of your life.

Chapter 5: Lucid Dreaming Techniques

Welcome to Chapter 5 of our book on Lucid Dreaming Techniques. In this chapter, we will be discussing the Mnemonic induction of lucid dreams (MILD) technique, Wake back to bed (WBTB) technique, Reality checks, Visualisations, Autosuggestion, and The Wake initiated lucid dream (WILD) technique. We will also talk about Dream reentry, Lucid living, and keeping a dream diary. By the end of this chapter, you should have a good understanding of all these techniques and how they can help you achieve Lucidity in your dreams.

Mnemonic Induction of Lucid Dreams (MILD)

The Mnemonic induction of lucid dreams is a technique that uses memory recall to induce a state of Lucidity during sleep. The aim is to plant the seed of awareness in your mind before falling asleep so that you will become conscious during the dream and be able to control its outcome. To do this, you recall a recurrent dream scenario that will trigger your conscious mind so that when you next experience this during a lucid dream, you will remember to become lucid.

To practice this technique, write down a list of words or phrases that remind you of a dream scenario from which you became lucid in the past. For example, if in the past you had a dream of flying above a city and a voice told you, "You are dreaming," then you can use the phrase "I am dreaming" to remind yourself to wake up and become lucid. Repeat this phrase to yourself for ten minutes before going to sleep.

When you next have that dream, hopefully, your subconscious mind will have been alerted to the possibility that you have become lucid and will be able to wake you up and cause you to become conscious in your dream.

How it Works

MILD works by creating cues that will remind you to become aware during the dream state. These can be mental or physical reminders, such as repeating a mantra before sleep, "Tonight I will remember my dreams", or placing an object by your bedside that you must look at when you wake up, for example, a photo of yourself. The dream scenarios you have recalled from memory associated with these cues will resurface during the REM phase of sleep when you become lucid. Their presence will alert your subconscious mind to the potentiality of being awake in the dream and help you break free of the dream-sleep cycle and wake up.

As you fall asleep, your subconscious mind will take over and begin to create the dreamscape. By using MILD, you are essentially training your mind to become aware that it is dreaming so that you can take control and manipulate the dream content when the dream begins.

Tips for Using Mnemonic Induction of Lucid Dreams

There are many tricks to mastering MILD. For example, to make sure you do not fall asleep immediately after repeating your phrase to remind yourself to become lucid, sleep next to a clock or calendar. This way, you will see when to repeat your phrase and time it with your breathing rhythm. Once you are asleep, you can close your eyes or keep them closed and think only of the phrase you've chosen. Keep practicing until you fall asleep and dream about the scenario and phrases you have set up to trigger your conscious awareness.

There are a few things to keep in mind when using MILD:

- It is important to create realistic dreams that could happen to you. This will make it more likely that you will believe the dream is real and become conscious during it.
- Make sure your chosen reminder is something you can't ignore! If possible, set multiple reminders, both a mental and physical one, so that there's no way you can forget.
- Place your reminder where you will see it as soon as you wake up: this will help jolt your memory and remind you of the intention to become lucid in the dream state.
- Be patient! This method takes a lot of practice and starts slow. Try it once or twice a night until you get the hang of it and can use it every night.
- It may take several nights of practice before seeing results, so don't get discouraged if it doesn't work immediately. Keep at it, and eventually, you should start having success with MILD.

The Mnemonic induction of lucid dreams is a powerful technique that can achieve Lucidity during the dream state. By planting reminders before sleep, you can train your mind to become aware of the dream and take control over its content. With practice, MILD can be an incredibly useful tool for anyone interested in exploring the world of lucid dreaming.

The Wake Initiated Lucid Dream (WILD) Technique

The Wake Initiated Lucid Dream technique is a powerful tool for inducing Lucidity in your dreams at any time of the day. By practicing WILD before going to sleep, you can become lucid in your dreams during any stage of sleep. This technique requires a lot of practice to perfect and can take time to learn; however, once mastered, it can be very useful for consistent lucid dreaming. If you struggle to consistently induce lucid dreams regularly, then this might be the lucid dreaming technique for you.

The Wake Initiated Lucid Dream technique works by waking yourself up during a dream and tricking your subconscious into believing you are awake. The idea behind WILD is that having your subconscious mind think it is awake will be more likely to cause you to become lucid during your dreams. Only a small percentage of people can naturally wake themselves up while dreaming, meaning that the chances of this type of lucid dreaming happening are fairly small. However, practicing the Wake Initiated Lucid Dream technique increases your odds of becoming lucid during your dreams, even during the more mundane stages of sleep.

The WILD technique involves going to sleep while remaining aware of your surroundings and keeping your mind focused on your intention to dream. As you drift off to sleep, you will enter the hypnagogic state, a transitional state between wakefulness and sleep. In this state, you will be able to maintain your awareness and focus on your intentions while asleep. In this state, you will be not only able to become lucid but also conscious of the fact that you are in a dream. You will then be able to take control of your dream and do whatever you want.

You may experience hallucinations or strange sensations as you enter the hypnagogic state. It is important to remain calm and focused and not allow these hallucinations to scare you. These are common experiences in the hypnagogic state and should not prevent you from experiencing lucid dreams. Once you have entered the hypnagogic state, you will want to focus on your intention to dream and have a positive view of lucid dreaming. This will increase your chances of experiencing lucid dreams.

In the dream state, you will be aware that you are dreaming and can control the dream. You can explore the dream world and interact with other dream characters. You will then experience awareness that you are dreaming and can control the dream.

There are a few things that you can do to increase your chances of success with the WILD technique:

- Keep a dream journal: Keeping a detailed record of your dreams will help you become more familiar with the dream state and make it easier to recognize when you are dreaming.
- Practice meditation: Meditation can help you develop focus and concentration, which will help maintain your awareness in the hypnagogic state.
- Make sure you are well-rested: Trying to induce a WILD when you are tired is likely unsuccessful. Make sure you get a good night's sleep before attempting this technique.
- Have a relaxed restorative sleep: Having a relaxing restorative sleep will improve the quality of your sleep and help you to fall asleep more quickly and more easily, which will make it easier to remain asleep when you attempt a WILD.
- Keep an open mind: Try to have a positive attitude towards lucid dreaming and keep your mind focused on lucid dreams. Have a positive expectation that you will

lucid dream and believe you will, rather than doubting your ability.

The WILD technique is an effective way to induce a lucid dream. By remaining aware of your surroundings as you drift off to sleep, you can enter a dream state while retaining your consciousness.

Wake Back to Bed

The Wake Back to Bed technique is a method of lucid dreaming induction that involves waking up after a few hours of sleep and then returning to bed. The idea behind this technique is that once you're awake and in the middle of the night, your brain is still producing delta waves. These are dreamless sleep waves that tend to linger throughout the night. By getting up only enough to go to the bathroom and return to bed, you can prolong the time you are exposed to delta waves and increase your chances of being lucid during your dream cycle. Faster sleep cycles are associated with REM sleep, and REM sleep is associated with vivid dreams.

To practice this technique, get up and go to the bathroom to give yourself a few minutes, then return to bed and lie down immediately again. When you wake up the next morning, ask yourself, "Was I dreaming?" and pay attention to your immediate response.

Wake Back to Bed usually sets the alarm for a few hours after falling asleep. When the alarm goes off, you wake up and stay awake for some time – anywhere from 30 minutes to 2 hours – before returning to bed. During this time, doing something beneficial will increase your awareness and make you more likely to remember your dreams, such as reading about lucid dreaming or keeping a dream journal. When you are done being awake, go back to bed and try to go back to sleep as quickly as you can. The idea is to go back to sleep while your brain is still producing delta waves and before it has slowed down to alpha waves associated with sleep. Sleeping during delta waves increases the chances of lucid dreaming since alpha waves are associated with deep sleep and REM sleep.

Some people find it helpful to drink caffeine during their Wake Back to Bed window, as caffeine can help improve alertness and memory recall; however, others find that caffeine makes them too restless to fall back asleep. There is no one "right" way to do Wake Back to Bed, so experiment until you find what works best for you.

Tips for Using Wake Back to Bed

If you are having trouble falling back asleep after waking up in the middle of the night, try reading a book about lucid dreaming or keeping a dream journal. It is a proven way to get better at lucid dreaming because these activities will help activate your right brain and open up your third eye.

If you can stay awake for 30 minutes to an hour without falling asleep, then go back to bed and try to rest for the remainder of the night. The less time you spend awake when your brain is still producing delta waves, the higher your chances of becoming lucid!

If you wake up in the middle of the night and cannot fall back asleep, try meditating for a few minutes to calm your mind and prepare yourself for a lucid dreaming session.

Another good way to prepare for a lucid dream is to "wake up" slowly and then lie in bed for a few minutes to meditate and prepare your body and mind for lucid dreaming. When you feel ready, close your eyes and try to fall asleep. This way, your mind, and body will be better prepared for a lucid dreaming session when you fall asleep later that night.

While the Wake Back To Bed technique may not work for everyone, it is one of the most popular methods of inducing Lucidity due partly to its simplicity. If you are interested in trying this method, give yourself enough time to wake up fully before attempting to go back to sleep – otherwise, you may just end up feeling groggy and disoriented!

The Fulfilment Box

The Fulfilment Box is a simple yet effective technique that can be used to induce lucid dreams. The idea behind this method is that by writing down your goals and desires before going to bed, you are more likely to dream about them – and hopefully achieve them. Even if you don't achieve the dream's objective, simply thinking about it while falling asleep can help trigger REM sleep and make you more likely to become lucid in the dream state.

To use the Fulfilment Box technique, simply grab a pen and paper, and write down what you want to dream about. It can be anything from meeting your favorite celebrity to winning the lottery – just make sure it's something you want! Once you have your list of dreams, put the piece of paper in a box or envelope and place it under your pillow before going to sleep. This is where it gets interesting: while you sleep, the subconscious part of your brain responsible for creating dreams is scanning your environment for things such as sight and smell. Through this process, the subconscious can pick up on your surroundings and latch onto your goal of becoming lucid in the dream. Then it will try to find ways to manifest your dream for you.

As you drift off into slumber, visualize yourself achieving each of the things on your list. See yourself crossing them off one by one until there's nothing left but accomplished goals. This will help plant the seeds for Lucidity in your mind and increase the chances of achieving those things in real life. Writing down things you want to accomplish in your future can help you break through mental roadblocks and achieve your goals more quickly.

This is a very powerful method for inducing lucid dreams because it combines visualization and subconscious manifestation to create an overall powerful shift in mindset that makes it easier to become lucid in your dreams.

There are no hard-and-fast rules when using the Fulfilment Box technique. Some people like to write their lists in the present tense as if they've already achieved their goals (e.g., "I am rich"), while others prefer the future tense (e.g., "I will win the lottery"). Experiment and see what gets results for you. If you do find yourself having bizarre dreams that seem disconnected from your written goals, don't worry. It just means that your dreams were processing your old subconscious thoughts and answering them as though you had already achieved them. The Fulfilment Box is an incredibly versatile technique that can help you achieve just about any goal in life, from losing weight to finding your soul mate. While this is not the main method of lucid dreaming, it can still be an extremely useful tool for those that would like to explore the concept of manifestation to further their dream goals.

The Symbol Technique

The Symbol Technique is a powerful lucid dreaming technique that can induce Lucidity. The technique involves choosing a symbol representing Lucidity, then repeating it repeatedly until it becomes ingrained in your subconscious mind. The idea here is that visualizing the symbol while falling asleep will help send a clear message to the subconscious that you are ready for a lucid dream and are willing to accept the experience.

When choosing your symbol, selecting something unique and memorable is important. Once you have selected your symbol, you must repeat it regularly until it becomes second nature. It is also helpful to write the symbols down in a dream journal to track your progress. The secret to repeating your symbol is to do it enough times that it becomes natural to say or think about your symbol without thinking about it too much. If the symbol you choose has negative connotations or associations, drop it and find another.

Once the symbols are firmly entrenched in your subconscious mind, they will act as triggers for Lucidity when you see them during a dream. When you see the trigger symbol during a dream, it should serve as a reminder to become aware of the fact that you are dreaming so that you can take control of the dreamscape.

The Symbol Technique can be a very effective method of inducing Lucidity and can be easily adapted to any dreamer's style. However, it is important to remember that this technique does not work for everyone and may take some practice to excel.

Reality Checks

Reality checking is a technique to increase the likelihood of lucid dreams. The idea behind reality checking is that if you can question the reality of your surroundings during the day, you will be more likely to do so in your dreams. By practicing reality checks during the day, you can perform a reality check during a lucid dream and realize that you are dreaming.

This is an effective method of becoming lucid because it allows you to take conscious control of your dream while realizing you are experiencing a dream at the same time. This combination of awareness and control will cause you to snap out of the dream and return to your physical body, allowing you to wake up and start a new dream cycle.

Reality checking involves regularly questioning the reality of your surroundings during the day.

There are many different ways to reality check, but some common ones include:

- Asking yourself whether you are dreaming or not
- Looking at a clock or watch to check the time: time often behaves oddly in dreams.
- Trying to push your finger through your palm: things can pass through hands in dreams.
- Reading texts: words and letters often change in dreams.
- Asking yourself where you are: often, people will find themselves in places they have never visited before or in strange surroundings during the daytime.

Interestingly, reality checks are much more effective if you perform them during waking hours rather than at night before sleep. Research shows that reality checks performed before sleep can disrupt sleep and make it harder to fall asleep, so it is best to stick to practicing them during the day.

Finding a reality check that works for you is important, as this will make it more likely that you will remember to do it in your dreams.
Experiment with reality checks and find the one that works best for you personally. The key is to practice them regularly during the day and to take some time before bed to remind yourself that you are dreaming before going to sleep.

Reality checking is a useful technique for increasing the likelihood of having a lucid dream. By regularly questioning the reality of your surroundings during the day, it is thought that you will be more likely to become aware that you are dreaming when in fact, you are.

Visualizations

Visualizations are mental images that you create in your mind. To use visualizations for lucid dreaming, you need to be able to control and manipulate the images you create. The more realistic and vivid the image, the better. Visualizations help you to train your brain to look at your dreams as realities rather than things you should ignore or forget upon waking.

Visualizations are powerful lucid dreaming techniques and are a great way to increase your odds of becoming lucid in your dreams. They are particularly useful for dreamers that cannot practice reality checks regularly during the day. Visualizations can be applied to every kind of dream and become much easier to visualize with the help of the Precognition Technique or Mental Replay technique.

The idea behind visualizations for lucid dreaming is that if you can control your dreams, then you should be able to control what you dream about. Suppose you have a strong enough imagination with practice. In that case, you can learn to induce Lucidity through visualization techniques alone, without relying on external aids like gadgets or supplements. This could give you complete control over your dreams and even turn them into reality.

There are many different types of visualizations, and you can choose whichever works for you. Common visualization techniques include:

- Visualizing Yourself in Your Dream: this will help you become more aware of your surroundings and help you recognize when you are in a dream.
- Visualizing Yourself in Your Body: this is helpful when trying to control your body in your dreams.
- Visualizing Lucidity: this technique involves visualizing yourself becoming lucid in your dream.

- Mentally Replaying Your Dreams: this technique involves mentally daydreaming about previous dreams to heighten your awareness of dreams.
- Mentally Replaying Your Night Before: this technique involves thinking about the events of your night before going to bed. This can help program your subconscious mind to expect a dream and allow you to become lucid more easily.

Visualizations are a powerful tool that can be used for lucid dreaming. With enough practice, anyone can learn how to use them effectively. By creating strong mental images of what you want to dream about, you can increase the chances of those images appearing in your dreams and reporting them as reality.

Autosuggestion

Autosuggestion is the process of using positive affirmations to influence your subconscious mind. This can be done through mental rehearsal or by repeating positive statements. When used in conjunction with other lucid dreaming techniques, autosuggestion can help increase the chances of having a lucid dream.

Autosuggestion is a relatively simple lucid dreaming technique that requires no special equipment. It is thought that you can use autosuggestion for lucid dreaming every night before bed by simply repeating positive statements to yourself about lucid dreaming. By repeating these statements repeatedly and with conviction, you can subconsciously condition your mind to want to be lucid in your dreams.

This is a useful technique that can be used in combination with other techniques to increase the odds of lucid dreaming. By repeating positive statements about lucid dreaming every night before bed, you can condition your subconscious mind to want to be lucid, making it easier to become lucid when you go to sleep.

Autosuggestion works by planting the seed of the desired outcome in your subconscious mind. The more you focus on achieving that outcome, the more likely it will happen. In the context of lucid dreaming, autosuggestion can be used to increase the chances of having a lucid dream. This is because when you repeatedly tell yourself that you will have a lucid dream, your subconscious mind is likelier to make it happen. People who repeatedly and confidently state that they will do something are much more likely to achieve it than people who doubt their ability to do it.

The key to effectively using autosuggestion is to say it confidently and repeatedly. Be sure to have a positive attitude and believe that what you say is true. If you have been saying positive affirmations about lucid dreaming for some time and still feel that you have yet to have a lucid dream, then you are not saying them with sufficient conviction, or you do not believe the words you are saying.

Dream Reentry

Dream reentry is a technique used to induce a lucid dream. It involves going back to sleep after waking up from a non-lucid dream and entering the dream again at the point where you woke up.

Dream reentry is a technique that can be useful for increasing the probability of having a lucid dream and is especially effective if you wake up regularly and have a restless sleep. By going back to sleep and entering your dream again, you are more likely to repeat the same dream and have a better chance of becoming lucid. It is a very simple and easy technique to increase your chances of becoming lucid, though many people do not know how to do it correctly.

Dream reentry is an easy technique that requires no special equipment or training. All you need to do is get out of bed within five minutes of waking up from a dream and go back to sleep. Once you have gone through the stages of sleep, you are more likely to enter the same dream again, giving you a chance to become lucid.

The idea behind dream reentry is that you are more likely to become aware that you are dreaming if you go back to sleep and enter the dream at the same time you woke up from it. This is because the dream memories will still be fresh in your mind, and you will be able to recognize the dream signs. Focus on the dream and try to reenter the dream as soon as possible. The sooner you enter the dream, the more likely you are to become lucid.

To do this technique, you need to set the alarm for a few hours after you usually sleep. When the alarm goes off, wake up and stay awake for about 5-10 minutes. Then, go back to sleep and try to enter the dream at the same point where you woke up from it. Try to remember the dream as much as possible and remember the scenes you witnessed in it. As you enter the dream again, focus on becoming lucid, and take control of your dream. If you wake up again, repeat the process until you are lucid in your dream.

Keeping a Dream Diary

Recording your dreams is an effective technique for inducing Lucidity. By keeping a dream diary, you are training your brain to become more aware of the dream state. In addition, the act of recording your dreams can also help to increase the recall of your dreams and your ability to remember details of your dreams after waking.

Keeping a dream journal is a very effective technique that can improve the recall and intensity of your dreams over time as you continue to practice it consistently. By writing your dreams down, you commit them to memory, making it more likely that your mind will remember them when it dreams again. In addition, by writing down more detailed information, you are conditioning your mind to be more self-aware and conscious about the dream state. With more conscious awareness comes better recall and more realistic dreams.

There are a few different ways that you can keep a dream diary.

- One way is to simply write down your dreams as soon as you wake up from them.
- Another way is to keep a notepad and pen by your bed so that you can jot down your dreams as soon as you wake up from them.

Whichever method you choose, it is important to be as detailed as possible when recording your dreams. Include as much information as you remember, such as the characters, setting, plot, and emotions felt during the dream.

Some dream journals come with special pages where you can take notes on your dreams, and in some cases, you can even record audio or video logs of your dream experiences. Dream journaling has been shown to have an incredibly positive effect on the recall of the dream state.

Tips for keeping a dream journal.

- Make sure to date each entry in your dream diary.

- It can be helpful to write down keywords or symbols that stand out to you in each dream entry. These will be easier to remember later on and can help trigger lucidity.
- In addition to writing down your dreams, it can also be helpful to draw pictures of them. This is especially useful for visual learners.

Keeping a dream diary is a great way to increase awareness of the dream state and induce Lucidity. Be sure to be as detailed as possible in each entry and consider using keywords or symbols to help trigger lucidity in future dreams.

Chapter 6: Preparing For Your First Lucid Dream Experience

Put Yourself in the Right Frame of Mind

Lucid dreaming is a mental state in which the dreamer is aware that he is dreaming. This awareness can occur both during and after the dream. Lucid dreams can be vivid and lifelike, feeling more real than real life at times. Lucid dreaming is a skill that can be learned and honed through practice, and it can be an enthralling and enjoyable experience. To prepare for lucid dreaming, you must first get into the right mindset and set lucidity goals. A positive mindset is one of the most important requirements for successful lucid dreaming. A success mindset is essential for feeling confident that you can achieve lucidity, stay lucid, and achieve your goals while dreaming. When you understand and believe in the possibility of lucid dreaming, you will set yourself up for success.

You must first determine your goals to achieve lucidity in your dream. What are your expectations for your dream? Which aspects of your life do you want to change or improve? Answering these questions will help you develop a plan and focus your efforts on achieving lucidity. When you've decided what you want to achieve, write it down or tell someone about it. Knowing what you want to achieve will allow you to concentrate your efforts on achieving lucidity. It is critical that your goal is realistic and achievable and that you have a clear plan.

It is essential to have realistic expectations for your first lucid dream experience. This will help you manage your expectations and avoid disappointment if your dream does not come true. Remember that everyone's first lucid dream is unique, and there is no right way to achieve lucidity. Be patient and do not expect perfection right away.

Patience is one of the most important things to remember when preparing for your first lucid dream. It takes time, practice, and patience to learn how to lucid dream. You must persevere in your efforts and not give up if you do not see immediate success. Be willing to try new techniques until you find the ones that work best for you. Remember that mistakes are part of learning and the path to successful lucid dreaming.

A positive attitude is necessary for success in any endeavor, but it is especially important when learning lucid dreaming. Having faith in yourself and your ability to achieve lucidity is critical. Maintain a positive attitude and believe in your ability to succeed. When you maintain a positive attitude, you are more likely to act and persevere in facing setbacks. A positive attitude is essential for success in any endeavor, including learning how to lucid dream.

It is critical to have fun and enjoy yourself when learning how to lucid dream. The most important thing is to keep an open mind and say yes to opportunities as they present themselves. Try out different techniques to see which works best for you, and have fun while at it. Having fun and relaxing are important parts of the learning process and will keep you motivated to achieve your goal of lucidity. Maintaining a relaxed attitude as you learn lucid dreaming will make it easier to accept new experiences and the "weirdness" associated with dreaming. Finally, remember that practicing for fun and enjoyment is the best way to learn and concentrate on the process rather than the outcome. Make whatever techniques you try enjoyable for yourself.

You need to be willing to fail in any new endeavor. Learning to lucid dream is no exception. Prepare to make and learn from mistakes. We learn and grow as a result of our mistakes. Be patient with yourself, and don't expect immediate perfection. Allow yourself the freedom to experiment and discover what works best for you. Failures are part of the learning process for lucid dreaming and demonstrate your willingness to keep experimenting and trying new approaches when your current approach isn't working for you. Accepting failure as a necessary part of the process will help you not give up easily and improve your learning process.

There will be times when you must give up, tho. This is especially true if you have a nightmare or a bad dream. Knowing when to stop and wake up if you find yourself in a situation that causes you anxiety or fear is critical. You may need to remind yourself repeatedly that "waking up" is okay and that a nightmare will not harm you. Knowing that you are not in danger in your dream will help you recognize when you may need to "wake up" and regain full awareness. This will keep you from becoming too distracted or frustrated while experimenting with new lucidity methods.

Select a Lucidity Technique That Suits You

There are several techniques for inducing lucid dreaming. Each technique has benefits and drawbacks, so it is critical to find one that works best for you. Some techniques are more effective for certain people than others, so you should experiment to find the one that works best for you. The most important aspect of your efforts is to be patient and persistent. Don't give up if you don't see immediate results.

Some people prefer learning new concepts by reading about them, while others prefer watching videos or listening to audio recordings. Some people prefer to experiment independently, whereas others prefer to be guided by a teacher or coach. There is no single correct method for learning to lucid dream. Finding a learning style that works for you will help you learn more effectively and achieve better results. Many online quizzes can help you determine your learning style if you are unsure. Once you've identified your learning style, you can select the technique that will work best for you.

Once you've decided on a technique, you should put it to use regularly. The more you practice, the more likely you are to succeed. Remember to be patient and don't expect instant gratification. Maintain a positive attitude and have fun with the process.

Learning to lucid dream takes time and practice, just like any other skill. You may not see immediate results, but it is critical to persevere in your efforts.

If one technique isn't helping you achieve clarity, try combining it with another. Some believe combining several techniques is more effective than just one. Experiment to find the best combination of techniques for you.

Using anchoring techniques to remind you to perform reality checks is one way to increase your chances of becoming lucid in your dream. Reality checking is a technique for determining whether or not you are dreaming. It entails searching for inconsistencies in your dream environment and seeing if you can control your actions in the dream. Anchoring techniques entail creating a physical or mental trigger to remind you to perform a reality check when you see it in your dream. You could, for example, set a phone reminder to go off every hour, or leave a note on your bedside table that says "reality check."

One of the most effective ways to increase your chances of having a lucid dream is to keep a dream journal. A dream journal is a record of your vivid and mundane dreams. Writing down your dreams makes you more aware of them and increases the likelihood that you will remember them when you wake up. Writing down your dreams also helps you notice patterns and themes in your dream life. These patterns can be used to increase the likelihood of becoming lucid in your dreams.

Affirmations are positive statements that assist in programming your mind for success. When used regularly, affirmations can help boost your confidence and motivation, increasing your chances of reaching your goals. Affirmations can be used with other techniques such as dream journaling and reality checks. Affirmations are an easy way to improve your chances of success in lucid dreaming.

Create a dream-friendly environment.

Getting enough sleep is important to prepare for lucid dreaming. Dreams happen during the REM (rapid eye movement) stage of sleep, which happens after about 90 minutes. Most people require approximately 7-8 hours of sleep per night to feel rested and refreshed during the day. It will be more difficult to achieve lucidity in your dreams if you do not get enough sleep.

Eating healthy foods and exercising regularly are important for overall health and well-being, but they can also aid in dream lucidity. Eating a healthy diet improves sleep quality, making it easier to achieve lucidity. Exercise can also help improve sleep quality and reduce stress and anxiety, which can aid in achieving and maintaining lucidity.

Stress and anxiety can make achieving lucidity in your dreams difficult. If you are stressed or anxious, try to find ways to relax and reduce your stress. Yoga, meditation, and deep breathing exercises are some relaxation techniques that may be beneficial. Reduced stress and anxiety will make you feel more relaxed and increase your chances of attaining lucidity.

Developing a relaxing bedtime routine is an excellent way to prepare for sleep and reduce stress. Taking a warm bath, reading a book, or listening to soothing music can all be part of a relaxing bedtime routine. A consistent bedtime routine will help signal to your body that it is time to sleep, which can improve the quality of your sleep and make it easier to achieve lucid dreams.

Another important step in preparing for lucid dreaming is to make your bedroom comfortable and conducive to sleep. Cool, dark, and quiet is the ideal sleeping environment. To block out light, use blackout curtains or an eye mask; to block out sound, use earplugs or white noise. Creating a relaxing environment will assist you in falling asleep more easily and improving the quality of your sleep.

Going to bed and getting up at the same time every day aids in regulating your body's natural sleep cycle. This can improve your sleep quality and make achieving lucidity in your dreams easier. A regular sleep schedule will also help you feel more rested and energetic during the day.

If you have trouble sleeping, many supplements and medications can help. Melatonin and valerian root are two supplements that can help you sleep better. If you are having trouble sleeping, your doctor may advise you to take Ambien or Lunesta. Because these medications can be addictive and have side effects, they should only be used as a last resort.

Some devices claim to aid in the induction of lucid dreams. Typically, these devices function by providing sensory stimulation during REM sleep, which is when dreams occur. If you decide to try one of these devices, carefully read the instructions and use it as directed.

Be prepared for setbacks.

Bad experiences are part of the learning process for any new skill. Don't get discouraged if you have a bad experience with lucid dreaming. Be patient and don't expect perfection right away. Allow yourself to make mistakes so that you can learn from them. The more you practice, the better you will become at lucid dreaming.

Sleep paralysis is a condition that can occur during or after sleep. It is characterized by an inability to move or speak while awake. Sleep paralysis can be a frightening experience, but it is not dangerous. It is important to be prepared for sleep paralysis if you are planning to attempt lucid dreaming. There are several ways to prepare for and deal with sleep paralysis, including relaxation techniques and visualization exercises.

Bad dreams or nightmares can occur during any stage of sleep. They are more common during REM sleep when most dreams occur. Nightmares can be caused by stress, anxiety, or medications. If you are having nightmares, it is important to have a plan for dealing with them.

If you find that your nightmares are causing you distress or interfering with your daily life, it is important to seek professional help. A therapist can help you deal with the underlying causes of your nightmares and provide you with tools to deal with them.

Lucid dreaming, drugs, and alcohol can be dangerous and should be avoided. These substances can interfere with your sleep, cause nightmares, and increase the risk of sleep paralysis. If you are taking medication for a mental health condition, it is important to talk to your doctor before attempting to use any substance to induce lucid dreaming.

Several devices claim to induce lucid dreaming. However, there is no scientific evidence that these devices are effective. Some of these devices can be dangerous, so it is important to use caution if you decide to try them.

Lucid dreaming can be a thrilling and exciting experience. However, there are some risks associated with it. These risks include sleep paralysis, nightmares, and false memories. It is important to be aware of these risks before attempting to induce lucidity in your dreams.

Set aside your expectations.

Expect to be unable to lucid dream on your first attempt. Developing the skill of lucidity takes time and practice. It takes time to learn and master, just like anything else. The more you practice lucid dreaming, the better you will become. So don't expect to be an expert right away. You may become frustrated if your first attempts do not go as planned, but persevere, and you will improve with practice. Practice is what will improve your lucid dreaming abilities, so keep working on improving your lucid dreaming abilities, and your success rate will rise.

What works for one person may not work for another. Experimenting with different techniques is the best way to learn how to lucid dream. Find a technique that works for your learning style and put it into practice regularly. Whatever happens, be persistent and never give up on your dreams. If one technique doesn't work for you, try combining them or using anchoring techniques (such as counting backward from 10) to help you remember to perform reality checks during the dream.

There is no guarantee that any particular technique will be effective for everyone. Some people excel at visualization, while others prefer cognitive restructuring techniques such as focusing on positive thoughts or affirmations before bedtime. The key is trying different things and seeing what works best for you. Don't be discouraged if you don't see immediate success; patience is essential when learning anything new. Just keep practicing, and you'll get better at lucid dreaming!

Just like in real life, there will be times when things do not go as planned when attempting to lucid dream. Don't be discouraged; this is all part of the process of successfully learning to lucid dream. Be willing and open to trying new techniques until something sticks and starts producing consistent results for you. You'll eventually be successful at lucid dreaming if you're patient, have fun, and stay focused on your goals.

Remember that just because you don't succeed the first time you try to lucid dream doesn't mean you're a failure. Just keep practicing, and you'll eventually find a technique or combination of techniques that works for you. If things don't go as planned, don't be discouraged; it's all part of the learning process. And keep in mind that no matter how good your intentions are, there is always room for improvement regarding lucid dreaming abilities.

Don't let discouragement or frustration keep you from pursuing your dreams. Learning to lucid dream successfully can take time, but with patience and perseverance, anything is possible! If something isn't working for you right now, be willing to try new techniques until something clicks – just like with any other skill or activity!

Lucid dreaming is a fascinating experience that anyone can enjoy. Remember to have fun while learning how to lucid dream and that it is a continuous process that will require time and practice to master. Simply relax, concentrate on your objectives, and believe in yourself; success is within reach!

Look for progress rather than perfection.

Recognize that there is no perfect method. There is no one way to lucid dream that is perfect. There is no one way to be successful in life, and there is no one way to have lucid dreams. Keep in mind that progress, not perfection, is the goal. This is an important concept to remember. To stay motivated and focused on your goals, let go of your expectations of perfection.

Don't dwell on your mistakes. Failure is a necessary part of the learning process. Remember that every dreamer has varying degrees of success and failure when attempting to lucid dream. Simply keep practicing, and you will eventually succeed. Instead of focusing on your failures, concentrate on your progress. Recognize your progress and maintain a positive attitude in the face of setbacks.

Celebrate your accomplishments, no matter how minor. Celebrate when you finally succeed at lucid dreaming! Take time to appreciate your accomplishments, no matter how minor they may appear at first. Pat yourself on the back for being persistent and open to new experiences. Remember that even small steps forward can lead to big achievements later on.

Be patient and don't expect instant gratification. When you first begin attempting to lucid dream, your skills may take time to develop. Don't give up on your dreams because things haven't gone exactly as planned. Practice, like everything else in life, makes perfect. Persevere despite setbacks and keep trying until you achieve success. Lucid dreaming is a skill that takes time to master, but with perseverance and dedication, you can achieve success.

Be adaptable and willing to try new things. Don't be afraid to experiment with new techniques. As you practice, you may discover that certain techniques work better for you than others. Be open-minded and willing to try different methods to find the one that works best for you.

Maintain a positive attitude. Remember to keep a positive attitude when things get tough. Remember that learning new skills takes time and effort, but patience and dedication make success possible. Maintain your motivation by focusing on your successes rather than your failures. Remember that making mistakes is a necessary part of the learning process; do not become discouraged or frustrated.

Have fun and take in the scenery. Lucid dreaming is a fun experience that anyone can enjoy. Remember to have fun while learning and to be gentle with yourself when things get tough. Maintaining a positive attitude and staying motivated throughout the process is critical.

Reward yourself for your accomplishments.

Celebrate your accomplishments and give yourself credit for your hard work, whether you achieve a minor goal or something more significant. This will assist you in staying motivated and on track. It's also important to remember that success doesn't come easily – becoming a lucid dreamer takes time, effort, and practice. Allow yourself to have some fun while learning!

Smaller goals will keep you focused and motivated. When you achieve a goal, take the time to celebrate your accomplishment. This does not have to be anything major; simply take some time to relax and enjoy the moment. Celebrating your accomplishments will keep you on track and motivated in future endeavors.

There are numerous ways to recognize and reward yourself for your efforts. Some people prefer monetary or gift certificates as rewards. Others enjoy relaxing by going on vacation, spending time with friends and family, or simply engaging in a favorite hobby. Whatever you decide, make sure it will make you happy and help you stay motivated.

Take a break if you are feeling overwhelmed or stressed. Don't try to do too much at once; instead, set aside time to relax and rejuvenate. Return when you're ready to continue honing your lucid dreaming abilities.

Don't give up and keep trying. Continue to try even if you haven't had success with a particular technique in the past. Because every dreamer is unique, what works for one person may not work for another.

Have fun while learning; this will make the process more enjoyable. Remember that lucidity is a skill, like any other, and that you should enjoy the process of learning and mastering it.

Chapter 7: Inside a Lucid Dream

You can explore higher states of consciousness through lucid dreaming if you have the skills to maintain your lucidity, prevent yourself from waking up before you want to, and steer the dream in a helpful direction. Lucid dreaming is one of the most interesting and unique ways to experience life outside of the body. It's like being in two places at once: while you're dreaming, you're fully conscious and able to control your dreamscape; but when you wake up from a lucid dream, all traces of that controlled environment are gone, leaving you with an enduring memory of what happened during the dream.

Stronger Lucidity

To stabilize lucidity, focus on your goals. Beginners should have a clear goal before bed each night to help them create a more meaningful dream. Knowing what you're working towards will make you more likely to stay focused and achieve your dreams' objectives. By establishing a goal before sleep, you'll also reduce the likelihood of having unproductive or irrelevant dreams. Make sure your goal is something that interests you and that challenges you. It should be something that makes you feel excited and motivated to continue striving for it. As with anything else in life, practice makes perfect; over time, the easier it becomes to stay focused on your goals while dreaming. But even if things don't go perfectly at first, keep trying. The most important thing is that you're taking deliberate steps toward achieving your goals in dreams.

Postpone awakenings: if you feel your body spinning or your hand rubbing, remember that you are dreaming. Try to postpone waking up by continuing to spin your dream body or vigorously rub your dream hands together. If you sense that you're awake, conduct a reality check to be sure. Remember, having a clear goal before sleeping each night is important to have more productive and meaningful dreams.

Spinning your dream body: In a lucid dream, whirl your dream body as fast as you can to find a new dream scene. If you wake up, lie still and keep spinning. This will help induce a WILD. Spinning your dream body can also help you to focus on your dream environment. It seems like a silly thing to do, but spinning really does help. You will feel a sense of dizziness and may even see colorful lights. If this happens, it means you are close to lucidity.

Hand Rubbing: When you imagine yourself using one of your five senses, you're less sensitive to perceptions of your physical body lying still in bed. So if you sense that you're about to wake up, vigorously rub your dream hands together and try to fall back asleep while imagining the sensation of hand-rubbing for at least a minute. This will help reduce the chance of false awakenings. Rubbing your hands together has also been known to help induce a WILD, because the intense stimulation will cause your brain to release natural chemicals that are associated with dreaming.

Remembering that you are dreaming: Repeat the phrase "it is a dream" to yourself every few seconds while lucid dreaming reminds you of your state. This will help stabilize lucidity and keep false awakenings at bay. While you're lucid, it's also a good idea to take inventory of your surroundings and imagine interacting with any objects or people you see. This can help you learn more about the dream and deepen your immersion. When you are immersed in the dream and aware of it, repeat the phrase "I am dreaming" to yourself to increase your sense of control. This will help you focus on the task and stay grounded in the dream.

Practicing meditation during lucid dreaming: Lucid dreaming is a great opportunity to practice mindfulness and other forms of meditation. When you're in a dream, it's easy to focus on the experience rather than your thoughts and worries outside the dream. So take some time each day to sit down and focus on your breath or a mantra, and you'll likely start having more lucid dreams.

Step back from strong emotions and mesmerizing beauty: When we encounter something emotionally charged or stunningly beautiful in our dreams, it's easy to get caught up in the moment and lose lucidity. So if this happens, take a step back and try to observe the experience dispassionately. Doing so will make you more likely to maintain control over the dream and not get swept away by its intensity.

Recognize false awakenings: These are dream scenes in which you have awoken in your bed. They can be tricky to distinguish from reality, but tell-tale signs usually give them away. For instance, in a false awakening, you may find that you can't move your body or that your surroundings are slightly off from how they are. If you're not sure whether you're in a false awakening or not, try conducting a reality check. If you can pass the test, you know you're still dreaming. If not, you've probably awoken and should start your day.

Conduct a reality check: This is a test you can perform to determine whether you're awake or still dreaming. There are many different ways to do it, but one of the most common is to look at your hands and count your fingers. In a dream, your hands may appear distorted or have an abnormal number of fingers. Another reality check is to try to push your finger through your palm. In a dream, your hand will usually go right through.

These are all good tips that can help you postpone or determine whether you are awake or in a false awakening. Make good use of the above tips and you'll be on your way to a more lucid dreaming experience.

Exercise control

Lucid dreams allow you to see how your mental models of the world manifest in dream content. It is not uncommon for people to have a lucid dream after experiencing overwhelming situations of the day. While trying to exercise control in a dream state, you will find yourself remembering and identifying with other aspects of your life that you haven't used in some time. Focus on a specific aspect of your life that you wish to change your perspective or improve emotionally. Focus on the sensations you feel in your body when focusing on this problematic area; for example, what feelings come up when you think about your relationships with your parents or children?

Practice changing your dreams

Lucid dreams allow you to see how your mental models of the world manifest in dream content. Practice changing your dreams by walking through walls, making items vanish, manipulating objects' size, quantity, form, or speed, or entering someone else's body. Lucidity allows you to explore the possibilities of what your mind can create. Changing your dream is an exercise that teaches you to identify with your mental models of the world. As you do, you will also become aware of the beliefs that form the basis of your reality. This helps you let go of limiting beliefs and replace them with empowering ones. For example, part of the process of change may consist of:

- Accepting your limiting belief
- Identifying and accepting your alternative belief
- Embodying your alternative belief by consciously acting on it
- Changing your behavior pattern.

As you practice this in your dreams, you can add skills to your toolbox for changing your life by altering your beliefs. You will naturally identify and let go of limiting beliefs by replacing them with empowering beliefs. You will start to change your behavior and patterns in your waking life. For instance, you may identify a limiting belief and an alternate empowering belief related to your health. Then you may imagine that you are healthy and strong in your dream. With practice, you may walk into your dream and touch something in the dream that represents health to you. This creates a bridge between your waking life and your dream life, so the information you dream of may also come into your waking life.

Increase positive emotions

Using your lucidity to explore your mind's wonders lets you have more adventure and fun. Observe blooming flowers, and travel through unexplored lands and dreamscapes. Fly through waterfall-lined valleys, sail through the crystal waters, meditate in a sacred temple, and converse with an animal. Create art in your dream or dance in a temple of worship. Imagine flying higher than Mount Everest or swimming with sea life before diving to a dreamy beach. Lucidity can take your mind to the shore of inspiration, where creative solutions bubble up. You can choose whatever reality you want in lucid dreams: a serene place or a fresh adventure. Increasing positive emotions helps you let go of negative patterns, vibrations, and emotions limiting you. Changes include becoming more open and relaxed, having increased creative energy and enthusiasm, and having more joy and fun in life.

Skill rehearsal

Humans have evolved "imaging" abilities that allow them to rehearse responses to situations in ways that help them thrive. Humans can also create internal simulations that help them rehearse for important events, like performances, public speaking events, medical exams, interviews, or athletic events. You can use your dreams to explore issues in your daily life, such as relationships, emotions, health, finances, or greater society. As you learn to apply lucid dreaming skills in your daily life, you will naturally apply those skills during waking situations where you can use those new skills. Imagination is an amazing skill that humans have developed. When you use your imagination, you activate the inner senses that help you to experience reality differently. In lucid dreams, your imagination gets a boost because you create and control your reality. You can imagine anything—makeup that glows in the dark or flying through the sky on the back of a dragon. Lucid dreaming is an activity that puts you in touch with your hidden mental resources and helps you gain insights about your life as well as your dreams.

Creative problem solving

Lucid dreams are an effective way to practice problem-solving skills. Lucid dreamers report solving problems they encounter in their daily lives in dreams. Lucid dreamers also use dream explorations to solve problems they encounter —such as losing objects or coming across challenges—and find effective ways to handle these situations in their dream reality and waking reality.

Increased Self-Integration

Self-integration is a concept that has been described throughout human history. In Plato's allegory of the cave, humans lived in an underground cave their entire lives. Their vision was two-dimensional, and they were only allowed to see shadows of the world above. They had no idea that beyond the cave was a beautifully lit world where the objects were three-dimensional. Then one day, a man escaped the cave and showed his fellows that there was more to the world than the shadows and reflections they saw in the cave. A common misconception is that self-integration refers to a state of aloofness or introversion. If that were the case, we would all benefit from being on "hiatus" from society and getting off the grid. However, self-integration does not mean introversion or withdrawal. On the contrary, it requires being open to engaging with others and yourself. In the lucid dream state, you can learn how to integrate all aspects of your personality to improve your relationship with yourself and others.

Dream archetypes are universal symbols seen in lore across cultures, religions, and history. In dreams, archetypes can be characters, objects, settings, storylines, and other elements, such as an apocalyptic flood, your inner hero, or a mother and child. For example, in the Hindu religion, an archetype is Brahman, the universal force behind all creation. The Brahman nature exists within everyone and everything and is connected to all other natures. Even if we do not identify as Hindu or believe in Brahman, most of us can relate to the power of the archetypes depicted in these sacred stories. We all have an archetype that is connected directly with all of nature. The dream state is an amazing portal to understanding these universal symbols and how we can use them in our lives.

If you interpret your dreams while still dreaming, you can interact with them with greater intimacy and intellect and foster a greater understanding of how dreams work.

While dreaming in the lucid dream state, you can interact more fluidly and freely with other people and objects in your dreamworld than during a regular dream. By paying close attention to your feelings and emotions while dreaming, you can distinguish between real and perceived experiences. By being mindful and observing your perceptions while dreaming in a lucid state, you'll be better able to distinguish the real from the imaginary and increase your awareness of how your dreams work.

In the lucid dream state, you can practice self-exploration in various ways. You can practice looking in mirrors and exploring new environments and locations. You can also practice taking other actions in your dreams and observing yourself as you do them. These practices can help you become more self-aware and increase your mental clarity. By practicing self-exploration in your dreams and mindfulness while awake, you can better understand your internal and external worlds.

Positive dialogues: Lucid dreaming can help you engage hostile dream characters in conciliatory dialogues that promote healing and personal transformation. Through dreaming, you can also practice positive dialogues with troublesome people in your life. Communicating with your perceived enemies in lucid dreams is empowering, and having them respond positively to your words. You can have dialogues with difficult people in your life that contribute to the healing process. By practicing positive dialogues in your dreams, you can develop real-life communication skills and conflict resolution abilities.

Be friendly and curious: Remember you are in a safe environment in your dreams. By being friendly and relaxed in your dreams, you can interact with dream characters more relaxedly and activate your more cooperative and wise states of consciousness.

Ask questions and practice compassion: Dream characters reflect your mind, so be kind and compassionate to them. Try to see things from their perspective by asking questions about their role in your unconscious mind and psyche. Dream characters often reflect our own minds, fears, or wishes. Remember, they are simply a reflection of your mind. They represent your fears and wishes, and desires. They represent your own "shadow self." So be kind and compassionate instead of reacting negatively and trying to attack or run from them. Try to make friends with them first. Ask them questions. The more friendliness and curiosity you can bring them in the dream state, the more likely they will reciprocate. It is essential to be mindful of your internal dialogue and the quality of your thoughts while dreaming in the lucid dream state.

Use Affirmations: Practice positive affirmations as you enter your dream state. You can also practice self-affirmations like "I am safe" or "I am in control." These verbal affirmations can help improve your thoughts, feelings, and perceptions in your dreams. Doing this will help you increase positive experiences and dream content in your lucid dreams. If you want to practice affirmations without words, you can visualize or imagine affirmations before you go to sleep.

There are many ways lucid dreaming can foster self-integration. Remember, self-integration is a lifelong journey that requires commitment, courage, and perseverance. It is a highly individualized process that requires you to tune into your intuition and inner wisdom.

Lucid Dreaming in Real Life

Parallels

Identify elements from your dreams that reflect real-life issues to develop a deeper, more meaningful dialogue between states. It can be as simple as looking for a character in your dream that represents someone you know in real life or a situation that feels familiar. Once you've identified the parallels, you can start to explore what they (and the dream characters) mean. You may also want to write down or record dreams for future reference. The symbolism in dreams is allegorical. It's up to you to understand the symbols, how they are utilized, and what they mean in the dream.

What is this person or situation trying to tell you? What are the implications of what's happening in your dream? What does it say about your relationships or about yourself? The answers to these questions can be found by talking to someone who understands dreams, such as a therapist or a dreaming guide. They can help you to understand the symbolism and meaning of what you're seeing, and how it applies to your life. By exploring the parallels between your dreams and real life, you can start to develop a deeper understanding of both.

For example, if you dream that your boss is yelling at you, exploring what that dream is really about might be helpful. What is your relationship with your boss like in real life? Are there any similarities between how they treat you and how the character in your dream treats you? What does that say about how you feel about yourself? By exploring these questions, you can develop a deeper understanding of your dream and your real-life relationship. If you find that the dream reflects some unresolved issues in your relationship, you can use the dream as a starting point for addressing those issues.

Similarly, if you have a dream about failing an exam, it might be helpful to explore what that dream is really about. What are your expectations for yourself? What are your fears around failure? What does that say about how you feel about yourself and your ability to succeed? By exploring these questions, you can develop a deeper understanding of your dream and your real-life relationship with failure. If you find that the dream reflects some unresolved issues around failure, you can use the dream as a starting point for addressing those issues.

A lucid dreaming practice commits you to setting intentions for how you will apply the state of lucidity in useful ways. It helps you approach problems and situations with more mental flexibility. For example, suppose you're having trouble making decisions in waking life. In that case, lucid dreaming can help you to clarify your intentions and explore all sides of a situation before making a decision. Lucid dreaming can also help you clarify your goals and priorities. The parallels between lucid dreaming and conscious waking life will help you to understand yourself, your goals, and your dreams.

Take control of your mind

By learning how to lucid dream, you'll develop greater control over your mind. That control will help you relax, clear, and improve your relationships. You'll also have the tools to explore your mind's mysteries and understand your waking life better. As you explore your dreams, you'll develop a deeper understanding of yourself and your goals. If you're struggling with anxiety or stress, lucid dreaming can help you to identify the root causes of those feelings and address them directly. And if you're dealing with trauma or difficult memories, lucid dreaming can help you to process those experiences in a safe and protected context. Learning how to lucid dream will help you develop the self-awareness, control, and insight necessary to navigate life's challenges with clarity and confidence.

Set intentions

By setting intentions for how you want to use lucidity, and taking responsibility for those intentions,you can start to live more in alignment with your higher self. Aligning with your authentic self means living in alignment with your highest values and ideals. Taking responsibility for your intentions means being accountable for your actions. It means having the courage to follow through when things get tough. It means having the courage to take responsibility for your choices and the courage to choose again when you make a mistake.

When you understand in lucid dreams that your reality is being constructed from your mental models of the world, it is easier to take responsibility for your experiences. If you don't like what you're seeing in your dreams, you can veer off onto another path and explore another possibility.

In lucid dreams, you can define and shape your experience. This way, lucid dreaming allows you to explore your mind and define reality. You have complete control over what you see, hear, and feel. Lucid dreaming helps you learn how to break free of limiting beliefs and habits. It helps you learn to choose thoughts and behaviors that serve you instead of holding you back.

This understanding can be incredibly empowering and help you approach problems in waking life with more confidence and clarity. By taking responsibility for your dream reality, you can start to create the life you want to live and veer off paths that aren't serving you.

For many people, learning to lucid dream is a lifelong journey. It's a practice; like any practice, it takes time and effort to develop. Each night, you can learn a new skill, such as how to control your emotions or become more aware and accepting of your emotions. Over time, these new skills can help you in waking life. With each lucid dream, you gain a deeper understanding of your mental models, which helps you better understand your waking life.

With time, you'll find it easier to discern which dreams come from your conscious mind and from your subconscious. In waking life, we form our habits, thoughts, and beliefs on a subconscious level. We don't always recognize the influence of our subconscious or understand how our subconscious thoughts influence our waking lives.

Chapter 8: Dealing With Fear In Lucid Dreams

Understanding the Fear-Motivated Behavior in Lucid Dreams

When you become aware that you are dreaming, it is not uncommon to feel a sense of fear. Fear is a natural emotion and it serves an important purpose. It is your brain's way of protecting you from danger. In the real world, fear motivates you to avoid dangerous situations. It helps you to stay safe.

However, in a dream, there is no real danger. The things that you are afraid of in a dream are not actually going to hurt you. They are just products of your imagination. So, why does fear still exist in dreams?

There are two main reasons for this. Firstly, when you become aware that you are dreaming, your brain is still in "sleep mode". This means that the part of your brain that controls logic and reason is not fully active. As a result, you may not be able to think clearly enough to realize that the things that you are afraid of in a dream are not real.

Secondly, even though the things that you are afraid of in a dream are not real, your brain still responds to them as if they were real. This is because the part of your brain that controls emotions (the limbic system) is more active during dreams than the part of your brain that controls logic and reason (the prefrontal cortex).

So, even though you may know on some level that the things that you are afraid of in a dream are not really going to hurt you, your emotions can still override this knowledge and make you feel scared.

The good news is that there are ways to deal with fear in lucid dreams. Here are some tips:

-**Try to relax**: When you feel fear start to creep into your dream, take some deep breaths and try to relax your body. This will help to calm your mind and make it easier to think clearly about the situation.

-**Talk yourself through it**: Once you have calmed down, try to talk yourself through the situation logically. Remind yourself that nothing in the dream can hurt you and that there is no need to be afraid.

-**Change the scene**: If talking yourself through the situation doesn't work, then try changing the scene altogether. Use your lucidity to take control of the dream and change it into something more pleasant or less frightening.

-**Face your fears**: Sometimes the best way to deal with fear is to face it head on. If there is something in particular that you are afraid of in a dream (e.g. heights, spiders, snakes), then try to confront it directly. This can be a great way to overcome your fears in waking life as well as in dreams.

-**Ask for help**: If you are struggling to deal with your fear on your own, then don't be afraid to ask for help from a dream guide or another dream character. They can provide support and guidance that can help you to overcome your fear.

Remember, the next time you find yourself feeling afraid in a dream, there is no need to panic. Just take a deep breath and remind yourself that it is only a dream. With a little bit of effort, you will be able to overcome your fear and continue on with your lucidity.

Countering the Fear-Motivated Behavior

One of the most challenging aspects of learning to lucid dream is dealing with fear. It is natural to feel some anxiety when you first start exploring this strange new world. After all, you are venturing into unknown territory, and it is normal to feel a little apprehensive about the unknown. The key is to understand that the fears you experience in a lucid dream are not real. They may seem very real, but they are not. Just like in a nightmare, your mind is creating these fears in order to protect you.

The best way to deal with fear in a lucid dream is to take control of the situation. Remember, you are in control of your dreams. You can choose what happens in your dream, and you can change the outcome of any situation. If you find yourself in a scary situation, take a deep breath and remind yourself that it is just a dream. Then try to change the scenario. Make the monster go away or turn the darkness into light. Whatever you do, don't let fear control you.

One of the best ways to deal with fear in a lucid dream is to face it head-on. Instead of running away from your fears, try to confront them. This may seem counterintuitive, but it can actually be quite helpful. By facing your fears head-on, you will gain a better understanding of what they are and why they are there. Once you understand your fears, they will no longer have power over you.

If you find yourself in a situation that scares you, try to stay calm and focus on what is happening around you. Observe your surroundings and look for anything that seems out of place or strange. Once you have identified what is causing your fear, try to change it. If there is a monster lurking in the shadows, make it go away by turning on the lights or using your imagination to create a different scene altogether.

It is also important to remember that fear itself is not necessarily a bad thing. In fact, fear can actually be quite helpful if used correctly. Fear can motivate us to take action and make necessary changes in our lives. Without fear, we would likely take far more risks than we should and put ourselves in danger unnecessarily. So if fear does have some benefits, how can we use it effectively within our dreams?

One way to use fear constructively within dreaming is by using it as a tool for self-exploration. When we face our fears head-on within dreams, we can learn valuable information about ourselves that we may be otherwise unable or unwilling to access. We can explore what our deepest fears are and why they hold such power over us. This type of self-exploration can be incredibly helpful in overcoming our fears and achieving greater self-awareness. Additionally, by working with our fears constructively within dreams, we can also learn how to better deal with them when they arise spontaneously outside of dreaming.

In conclusion, while fear may initially seem like something negative, it doesn't have to be viewed as such. Fear can actually be quite helpful if used correctly, both within dreams and outside of them. So next time you find yourself feeling afraid within a dream, instead of avoiding or running away from the source of your fear, try confronting it directly. See what valuable information or insights you may glean from the experience.

Working With Fear In Lucid Dreams

When you become aware that you are dreaming, it can be a very exhilarating experience. However, it is not uncommon for people to feel a sense of fear or anxiety when they realize they are dreaming. This is because the dream world can feel very real and it can be difficult to control what is happening in the dream. There are a few things that you can do if you find yourself feeling afraid in a lucid dream. First, try to remember that you are in control of the dream and that nothing can hurt you. If you are worried about something specific, such as falling or being chased, try to remind yourself that it is just a dream and that you will wake up soon. It can also be helpful to focus on your breath and to relax your body. If you find that your fear is getting too overwhelming, you can always try to wake yourself up by pinching yourself or counting backwards from 10.

It is also important to remember that not all dreams need to be interpreted literally. Sometimes our fears in dreams can be symbolic of something else that is going on in our lives. For example, if you are afraid of falling in a dream, it might symbolize feelings of insecurity or anxiety in your waking life. If you are being chased by someone or something, it might represent something that you are running from in real life.
Try to take some time to reflect on what your fear might represent before dismissing it entirely. It could be helpful to journal about your dreams or to talk to someone who is experienced with interpreting dreams. Keep in mind, however, that there is no one right interpretation for any given dream – so trust your gut and go with whatever feels most meaningful to you.

If you find that fear is preventing you from enjoying lucid dreaming or from exploring the full potential of the dream state, there are some things that you can do to work through your fears. One option is to **slowly expose yourself to the things that scare you** in small doses until they no longer hold power over you. For example, if heights make you anxious, start by dreaming about being on a small platform or ledge and work your way up gradually from there.

Another option is **imaginal exposure therapy**, which involves spending time visualize facing your fears while remaining calm and relaxed. This technique can help "desensitize" your brain so that when confronted with the actual situation (in this case, a scary dream), you will be less likely respond with fear.

Both of these options require some effort and practice but eventually, they can help lessen the hold that fear has over your dreams – and over your life.

Transforming Nightmares with Lucid Dreaming

Unresolved psychological conflicts tend to be symbolically represented in dreams. To understand what a dream is trying to tell you, it can be helpful to keep a dream journal and track any emerging patterns. If you have a recurring dream, there is likely some unresolved issue in your life that the dream is trying to bring to your attention. Dreams can be interpreted on many different levels, but they all ultimately point to some aspect of yourself that you need to work on. By understanding the symbolism in your dreams, you can gain insight into your psyche and begin to work through the issues that are causing you anxiety or stress.

One of the most common symbols used in nightmares is fear. Dreams can be interpreted as a way for your subconscious to communicate with you about something that is bothering you. If you have a recurring nightmare, some unresolved fear or anxiety will likely be buried inside you. By confronting the fear head-on in your dreams, you can begin to work through the underlying issue.

Another common symbol found in nightmares is violence. This could be anything from being attacked by someone to witnessing a violent crime. In many cases, this symbolizes some underlying issue causing you fear or anger. By identifying the source of the fear, you can address it head-on in your life.

Finally, dreams can also be used to communicate unresolved emotions. If you have a particularly difficult nightmarish dream, it may indicate an emotional issue you are struggling with. By analyzing the symbolism in your dream, you can gain insight into the source of your problem and begin to work on resolving it. Dream interpretation is an incredibly powerful tool for self-awareness and growth.

To transform nightmares with lucid dreaming, you must first become aware of when you are dreaming. One way to do this is to keep a dream journal by your bed and write down your dreams as soon as you wake up. As you become more familiar with the content of your dreams, you will start to notice patterns and themes that emerge.

Once you have identified when you are dreaming, it's important to focus on changing the dream's content. If your nightmare includes being chased by a monster, try running towards the monster instead of away from it. Alternatively, you could try flying away or using your imagination to create a protective barrier around yourself. The key is to change the dream scenario to empower you and make you feel in control.

Lucid dreaming can be an incredibly powerful tool for overcoming nightmares. By becoming aware of when you are dreaming and changing the content of your dreams, you can take back control of your sleep and transform negative experiences into positive ones.

How to respond to nightmares

All humans are wired to seek happiness and avoid pain and discomfort. The problem arises when we keep cycling between flight, fight, or freeze responses. In a nightmare, your body responds as if you're truly being threatened or attacked. Your heart rate will spike, adrenaline will flow, and your muscles will tense up to protect yourself. This response is automatic and can be very difficult to resist. However, trying to avoid nightmares may miss out on valuable information that could help you resolve the underlying conflict. If confronting the nightmare is too daunting or scary, consider using one of the four approaches to nightmares.

Avoid: If avoidance isn't an option, try to minimize at least how much harm the dreamer does in the dream. For example, if a dream character is threatening you with a weapon or making violent threats against you, don't do anything that would provoke them further. Pay attention to what's happening in the dream without involving yourself directly.

Confront and Conquer: This approach involves facing your fears head-on and directly challenging the monster or threat. Sometimes this means physically confronting the figure in your dream, while other times, it might mean talking back to them or provoking them until they leave.

Go with the Flow: This approach focuses on accepting whatever happens during the dream as part of a natural process that must be dealt with at some point. For example, if you're dreaming about falling off a cliff into the cold water below, don't try to fight against gravity or swim toward shore; go with the flow and allow yourself to experience fear and panic until you wake up from the nightmare.

Seek Self-Integration: Lastly, focus on seeking guidance from within yourself to understand what's happening in your dreams and make sense of them. Many people find comfort knowing they are not alone in their dreams and can access wisdom from within themselves regardless of how frightening or uncomfortable they may feel.

It's important to remember that there is no one-size-fits-all solution for dealing with nightmares. The best approach for you will likely vary depending on the content of your dreams and your personal preferences. Experiment with different techniques until you find an approach that helps you feel more comfortable and in control when faced with your fears in dreams.

The most important thing is not to be afraid of your nightmares. They are a natural part of the dreaming process and can be a helpful tool for understanding your fears and working through them in a safe and controlled environment. However, find that your nightmares are causing you distress or interfering with your sleep. It may be worth talking to a therapist or counselor who can help you explore the meaning of your dreams and develop healthy coping strategies.

Positive Affirmations – Part 1

Positive affirmations express the belief that a certain thing is possible. They can benefit anyone striving for a goal by teaching them to think positively. Some people read positive affirmations every day to achieve specific goals. You can benefit by repeating these simple statements to yourself to help you overcome negativity and succeed at your goals.

Repeating positive affirmations help you reach any goal you strive for by increasing your self-confidence, building a positive attitude, and boosting your determination. This helps you visualize your goal and realize the importance of reaching it. This can be any goal you have on your mind!

Affirmations can help you reach your goals faster as they are positive thinking. They involve repeating a phrase or statement until it becomes "second nature."

Now relax and calm down as you repeat each affirmation five times in a row for 2 minutes each. You will listen to the affirmation, and there will be a pause of 2 minutes after each affirmation to give you enough time to repeat the affirmation and let your brain process it.

I am the most Powerful Being in this Body.
In my dreams, I am free to express myself without limitation.
I am free to have experiences that I may explore in my dreams
I can go where I want in my dreams.
In my dreams, my creativity flows freely because I have full reign over my thoughts and actions.
My dreams pursue me.
I look forward to dreaming.
In dreams, I experience and can achieve anything I wish.
I welcome my dreams morning and night.

In the morning, my dreams help me in my life today.

In the evening, my dreams help me reconnect to who I am deep down inside.

I dream of my purpose and use this momentum to propel me to make my dreams a reality.

The night is mine.

It is my time to focus on being who I truly am and to live life with enthusiasm and passion.

I am the master of my dreams.

I can create whatever I can imagine.

I have the ability and wisdom to work through any challenges that may arise in my dreams.

I willingly engage in Lucid Dreaming to accomplish my goals and desires.

I welcome my dreams and enthusiastically accept all the amazing experiences I can have in my dreams.

I enjoy this powerful time and treasure it because I know it is of infinite value to me.

I wake up each morning looking forward to dreaming.

The universe supports me in all my endeavors

I trust in the universe and its ability to keep me safe during my nightly adventures and to guide me to my ultimate goals.

I am safe in my dreams.

I am safe and secure in my meditations.

I release all worries and concerns to enjoy the dream experience to the fullest.

I am open to receiving all the guidance I desire in my dreams.

I can learn lessons in my dreams more easily and effortlessly than when awake.

In my dreams, I create the reality I wish to create for myself and those around me

In my dreams, I have an unlimited ability to heal myself and others who need healing.

I am flexible and easily change my thinking to my choosing.

I am naturally calm and relaxed in my waking life, which naturally translates into my dreams' calmness and relaxation.

My mind is filled with positivity and dreams.

I can utilize the powers of my dreams to manifest solutions to the problems in my waking life.

I have a limitless reservoir of energy, and this energy is put to good use when I go to sleep at night.

I can manifest anything I can imagine in my dreams with ease and grace.

I use my imagination to create anything I want in my dreams.

I am in total control of my reality in my dreams, and every experience and emotion is blissful.

The universe offers me opportunities to explore my dream consciousness.

I gladly accept these opportunities to use quantum mechanics to manifest my dreams into reality.

My dream travels take me to places I never thought of or imagined.

I awaken feeling refreshed and lighter after a good night's sleep.

I have a deepening sense of connection to others and the universe.

My mind is clear and at ease as I peacefully return to my waking world.

I am at peace with my creative soul's desires and the time and energy required for fulfilling them.

My dreams create wonderful feelings within me, which are positive catalysts for my experiences in my waking life.

I seek to expand my consciousness and learn as much as I can about myself.

My dreams connect me with my deepest desires.

I allow myself the freedom to make mistakes in my dreams, realizing that there is never any failure in my dreams.

I emerge from my dreams filled with wisdom and compassion.

I emerge each morning with a renewed sense of purpose and passion.

I am grateful for all my gifts in this world, including being able to dream lucidly.

I cherish this gift and cannot imagine a life without dreams.

I dream abundantly, soaking up all the information that comes to me in my dreams.

Every day, I find ways to improve my lucid dreaming so that I get the most out of this experience in my life.

Every experience I have in my dream is another step in my journey toward creating the world I wish to live in.

With a positive and open mind, I am open and receptive to all the information I receive in my dreams.

I clean the house daily, ridding my life of negativity so I can be ready to clear my mind each night.

I create a sacred space for sleeping in my dreams and honor this space with deep reverence and love.

Every experience I have in my dreams is rich with understanding and wisdom.

Positive Affirmations – Part 2

Every experience is viewed with love and compassion.

My dreams are my happy place. No matter what I dream, I always wake up with joy and excitement.

I honor myself in my dreams with actions, thoughts, and feelings that make me feel great and good about myself.

My dreams are my most profound connection to who I am, and I am grateful to have these dreams in my life.

No matter how hard I try, I cannot change the nature of my dream mind

When I surrender to the infinite possibilities that exist in life, my dreams take me places I could never imagine going.

I have infinite opportunities when my mind is open.

I invite positive vibrations into my life and accept the information and guidance that comes my way.

I allow my dreams to reveal themselves to me

My dreams are a reflection of my deepest desires, and I am determined to achieve them.

I am open to dreaming every night, and I eagerly await each dream.

I have profound insights into my dreams that help me understand my life better.

I use my dreams to work through problems and figure out solutions.

I have regular Lucid dreams that allow me to explore different aspects of my life.

I am fascinated by my dreams and enjoy learning about myself through them.

My focus is on having positive, beneficial dreams that help me in my waking life.

I have complete faith in my ability to dream and to control my dreams.

I know that my dreams are a powerful tool that I can use to improve my life.

I am inspired by my dreams and motivated to achieve my goals.

I am proactive in my dreams, and I make decisions that are in alignment with my highest good.

I am confident in my ability to dream and to interpret my dreams.

I use my dreams to gain a deeper understanding of myself and my place in the world.

I am comfortable with myself and my dream mind.

I am safe and secure in my dreams.

I allow myself to be vulnerable in my dreams, knowing that I am protected.

I am excited to explore my dreams and to learn more about myself.

This is a beautiful world, and my dreams reflect the beauty of the world.

I am blessed with the ability to dream, and I cherish this gift.

I use my dreams to help me heal from my traumas.

I have forgiven myself for my mistakes, and I am now able to move forward in my dreams.

Nothing can stop me from dreaming.

I am powerful and in control of my dreams.

I absolutely love dreaming, and I am grateful for this amazing experience.

None of my dreams are negative.

They are all positive and full of love.

I live in a world that is full of love, and my dreams reflect this love.

My dreams are a reflection of my highest self.

I am always connected to my higher self in my dreams.

I receive profound guidance from my higher self in my dreams.

My dreams are a reflection of my soul's purpose.

I am living my soul's purpose, and my dreams reflect this.

I am grateful for my dreams and the guidance they provide.

My dreams are a sacred experience, and I honor them as such.

I am open to all the possibilities that exist in my dreams.

I have full faith in my ability to achieve anything I desire in my dreams.

The sky's the limit in my dreams.

I can achieve anything I set my mind to.

In my dreams, I am free to be myself.

I am confident and secure in my dreams.

My dreams are a powerful tool that I can use to improve my life.

I don't need anyone's approval to dream.

This is my dream, and I am in control.

I am the creator of my dreams, and I create my reality.

I am powerful, and I use my power to create my dreams.

I know that my dreams are a reflection of my highest self.

No matter what I dream, I always wake up feeling thankful for the experience.

I focus on having positive, beneficial dreams that help me in my waking life.

I allow my dreams to reveal themselves to me.

The world is my oyster, and my dreams are my pearl.

I am motivated and inspired by my dreams.

Guided Meditation

Begin by lying down, letting yourself get comfortable, ideally flat on your back with your spine straight, legs uncrossed, arms at your side, palms facing open, however, if that is not comfortable for you, make comfort your priority and when you're ready, lovingly close your eyes.

Tuning into your own inner landscape.

Feeling your breath.

Inviting it to flow as softly and naturally as it wishes.

Relaxing and allowing gravity to take over.

It's safe to let go.

To release into relaxation.

Now think about your intention for this practice.

Why do you want to lucid dream?

What is it that you hope to achieve?

Allow yourself to really feel into your intention.

And as you do, begin to see yourself in a dream.

It doesn't matter what the dream is about, simply that you are aware that you are dreaming.

And as you become aware that you are dreaming, you may begin to see the dream begin to change.

You have the power to change the dream.

You are in control.

And you may begin to fly, or to float, or to move in any way that you wish.

You may explore your dreamscape, or you may choose to simply relax and enjoy the experience.

Whatever you do, trust that you are safe, and that you are in control.

Begin to notice any feelings or sensations that you experience in the dream.

You may notice that you feel lighter than usual, or that you feel a sense of freedom and flexibility.

Allow yourself to explore these sensations, and to really feel into the experience.

Relax even more.

Feel your body.

It is light.

You are dreaming.

And as you become more aware of your dream, you may find that you can control it.

You may be able to fly, or to travel to different places.

Or you may simply choose to relax and enjoy the experience.

Whatever you do, trust that you are safe and that you are in control.

Trust what you are experiencing.

And begin to feel yourself merging with this imagery.

You see yourself as the dreamer and the dream.

And you may begin to feel almost a sense of blissful ease.

And nothingness at all, Almost.

You are able to control wherever the dream takes you.

And you may find that you can change the dream to whatever you wish.

You may choose to fly, or to travel to different places.

Or you may simply choose to relax and enjoy the experience.

You see people or creatures in your dream, and you know that they are a part of you.

You are safe.

You are in control.

You decide what happens in the dream.

And when you are ready to come out of this practice, do so by first letting your awareness come back to where your body is right now.

Imagining roots anchoring you to the Earth, growing all along.

Either your back, in the back of your body, if you're lying down on your back, or whatever other part of your body is currently facing the Earth.

Just imagine, from your current angle, many roots are growing out of you.

And deep into the earth.

Allow yourself to imagine you are discharging any excess energy down, down through these roots, and letting that energy nurture the Earth as you only hold on to that which is for your highest, most loving good for now, to carry with you.

Moving forward and begin to really feel your body here now, noticing the points of contact between you and the surface on which you are resting.

And when you are ready, very slowly roll your shoulders, wiggle your fingers and your toes.

And only when you're ready.

Take your time as you open your eyes back to the world around you.

Thank you, namaste.

MELISSA
GOMES

FREEBIES

AND

RELATED PRODUCTS

WORKBOOKS
AUDIOBOOKS
FREE BOOKS
REVIEW COPIES

HERE

HTTPS://SMARTPA.GE/MELISSAGOMES

Freebies!

I have a **special treat for you**! You can access exclusive bonuses I created specifically for my readers at the following link! The link will redirect you to a webpage containing all my books and bonuses for each book. Just select the book you have purchased and check the bonuses!

>> https://smartpa.ge/MelissaGomes<<

OR scan the QR Code with your phone's camera

Bonus 1: Free Workbook - Value 12.95$

This **workbook** will guide you with **specific questions** and give you all the space you need to write down the answers. Taking time for **self-reflection** is extremely valuable, especially when looking to develop new skills and **learn** new concepts. I highly suggest you *grab this complimentary workbook for yourself*, as it will help you gain clarity on your goals. Some authors like to sell the workbook, but I think giving it away for free is the perfect way to say **"thank you" to my readers**.

Bonus 2: Free Book - Value 12.95$

Grab a **free short book** with **22+ Techniques for Meditation**. The book will introduce you to a range of meditation practices you can use to help you develop your inner awareness, inner calm, and overall sense of well-being. You will also learn how to begin a meditation practice that works for you regardless of your schedule. These meditation techniques work for everyone, regardless of age or fitness level. Check it out at the link below!

Bonus 3: Free audiobook - Value 14.95$

If you love listening to audiobooks on the go or would enjoy a narration as you read along, I have great news for you. You can download the audiobook version of *my books* for **FREE** just by signing up for a FREE 30-day trial! You can find the audio versions of my books (depending on availability) at the following link.

Join my Review Team!

Are you an avid reader looking to have more insights into spirituality? Do you want to get free books in exchange for an honest review? You can do so by joining my Review Team! You will get priority access to my books before they are released. You only need to follow me on Booksprout, and you will get notified every time a new Review Copy is available for my latest release!

For all the Freebies, visit the following link:

>> https://smartpa.ge/MelissaGomes<<

OR scan the QR Code with your phone's camera.

I'm here because of you

When you're supporting an independent author,
you're supporting a dream. Please leave
an honest review by scanning
the QR code below and clicking on the "Leave a Review" Button.

https://smartpa.ge/MelissaGomes

Manufactured by Amazon.ca
Bolton, ON

33862104R00068